SEWING JEANS

THE COMPLETE STEP-BY-STEP GUIDE

JOHANNA LUNDSTRÖM

Copyright © 2020 Johanna Lundström

Author: Johanna Lundström

Interior design: Johanna Lundström

Cover design: Rhis Nauyac Bayucca

Cover Photo: Johanna Lundström

Main photography: Johanna Lundström

Additional photography: 123RF.com, Freepik.com, Pixabay, Anja Cederbom

Illustrations: Rhis Nauyac Bayucca, Vectorstock, Johanna Lundström

Text editor: Kylie Walker

Publisher: The Last Stitch
thelaststitch.com

ISBN: 978-91-639-6152-6

All rights reserved. No part of this publication may be reproduced or transmitted in any form without the written consent of the author.

Printed in Latvia

CONTENT

FABRIC _____ 9
    Fabric glossary   10
    Fabric guide   11
    Quick guide:
    Pick the right denim   15
    Caring for denim fabric   16
    Reasons why denim
    jeans are problematic   18
    Ways to make jeans
    more sustainable   19
    Cutting denim   20

PATTERNS _____ 23
    Jeans pattern pieces   24
    A guide to seam allowances   25
    Jeans style pattern changes   26
    Drafting a curved waistband   30
    How to fix common jeans fitting issues   32

TOOLS & NOTIONS _____ 39
    Sewing machine equipment   40
    Handheld tools   43
    Notions   46

SEAMS _____ 49
    Tips for topstitching   52
    Sewing flat-felled seams   56
    Stitching bar tacks   64

ASSEMBLY _____ 67
    Order of assembly   68
    Pressing denim   69
    Regular front jeans pockets   72
    Classic front and coin pocket   76
    Professional jeans zipper installation   84
    Jeans zipper with a fly facing extension   93

    Button fly installation   100
    Back pockets   110
    Back pocket placements   114
    Back pocket stitching   116
    Crotch, yoke and side seams   122
    Flat-felled yoke and crotch   126
    Rectangular waistband   130
    Sewing a curved waistband   136
    Triple-layer belt loops   142
    Twin-needle belt loops   144
    Coverstitch belt loops   146
    Coverstitch belt loops with folder   148
    Single stitch belt loop   150
    Attaching belt loops   154
    Belt loops inside the waistband   156
    Rivets   160
    Sewing buttonholes   163
    Flat top buttons   166
    Donut buttons   168
    Straight stitch jeans hem   170
    Chainstitched jeans hem   173
    Triple straight stitch hem   177

DISTRESSING _____ 180
    Threaded holes   181
    Open holes   182
    Frayed hem   183

TOOL KIT _____ 184
    Download the jeans
    pattern tool kit   185
    Instructions   186
    Index   188
    Resources   190

INTRODUCTION

Eager to sew your first pair of jeans, but perhaps feeling a little intimidated? Or are you already making jeans and want to take your skills to the next level to achieve a more professional look?

My aim with this book is guiding you through the entire process. From picking the best fabric and adjusting the pattern for a perfect fit, to helping you stitch together your best pair of jeans ever using clearly illustrated step-by-step tutorials.

I've been sewing jeans for over two decades, made a lot of mistakes and figured out a ton of things along the way. So this book is a compilation of the best tips and tricks I've amassed over the years so that you can dive right into the process and achieve excellent results, even if you don't have previous experience. Essentially the sort of jeans making book I wish was available when I began on my denim sewing journey.

Since I know that many of you are intrigued by professional jeans making, I've also consulted with jeans making experts during the book creation process so that you can sew jeans like a pro using home sewing equipment.

So let's begin making some jeans!

Johanna

CHAPTER 1
FABRIC

FABRIC GLOSSARY

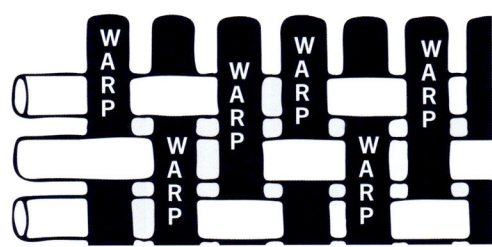

WARP
The indigo-coloured yarn that runs parallel to the selvedge. Warp yarns are predominantly seen on the right side of denim fabrics.

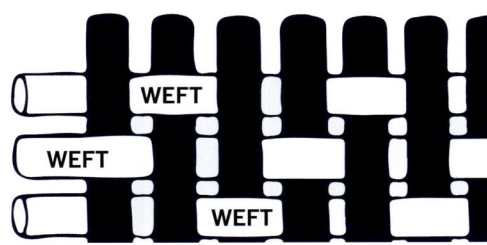

WEFT
The white (undyed) filling yarn that crosses the warp yarn, forming a pattern. The weft is mostly seen on the reverse side of the denim.

2X1 AND 3X1 DENIM
Denim weave consists of two or three indigo yarns and one white weft yarn on each repeat. 2X1 (shown) is lighter but still has a good weight for a pair of jeans. 3X1 denim is heavier and found in selvedge denim and more heavy-duty denim fabrics.

WEIGHT
Denim weight is calculated by its weight per square yard. Up to 12 oz is referred to as lightweight denim, 12–16 oz is medium weight and over 16 oz is heavy denim that's very stiff to wear and will need a lot of breaking in before it starts to soften. Today most jeans are made from denim weights ranging from 9–14 oz, with 12–14 oz considered classic denim weights.

INDIGO
A blue dye used for colouring the cotton yarns in denim fabrics. Initially, indigo was a natural dye mostly derived from the *Indigofera tinctoria* plant. But nowadays plant-based indigo has been replaced with synthetic versions.

FABRIC GUIDE

DENIM
A twill fabric traditionally woven with indigo blue warp yarns and a white weft thread. Due to the twill weaving techniques, the blue yarns are predominantly on the right side of the fabric, whereas the white weft is primarily seen on the reverse side.

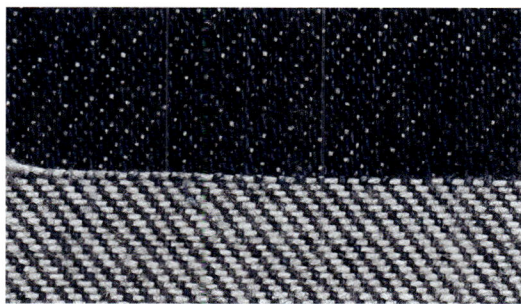

RIGHT-HAND TWILL
On the right side, the twill diagonals run from the lower left to the upper right. On the reverse side, the lines run in the opposite direction. This is the most common denim in modern manufacturing.

LEFT-HAND TWILL
The diagonal lines on the right side run from the lower right to the upper left. This type of denim twill is softer than right-hand denim.

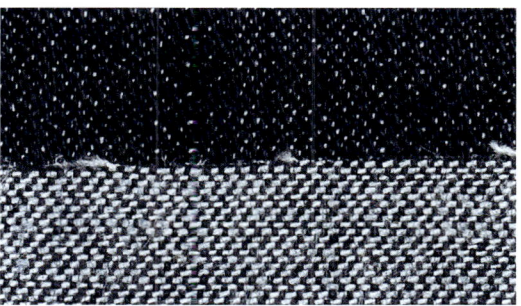

BROKEN TWILL
Broken twill is where the weave alternates to the left and right, forming a zigzag pattern. This weave prevents the denim from twisting, which is a common issue with regular right-hand denim.

STRETCH DENIM
Stretch denim has a small percentage of Lycra (Spandex) added, which improves the comfort and prevents the jeans from losing their shape. It is made of cotton/Lycra or a cotton/poly/Lycra mix, with the latter being a popular fabric choice for super skinny jeans because the added polyester prevents wrinkles and keeps the fabric from sagging.

RAW DENIM
Raw denim is a denim that hasn't been washed or distressed, which means it has a dark indigo colour and is fairly stiff. Jeans made of raw denim need to be broken in to be more comfortable, which means that they need to be worn for a long stretch of time to adjust to your body shape before washing.

TENCEL DENIM
Eco-certified Tencel/Lyocell denim is made of cellulose fibres. This fabric requires less water and is produced in a closed system with fewer chemicals compared with traditional cotton denim. Tencel is softer than cotton denim, so to achieve the firmness required of pants-weight denim, it's common to mix Tencel with cotton to create the right properties.

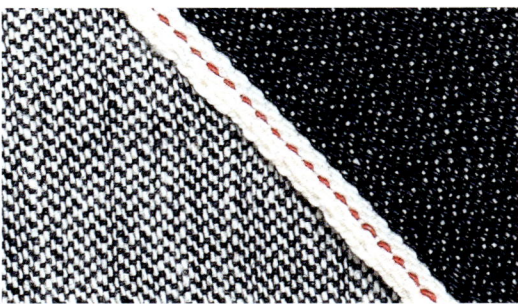

SELVEDGE DENIM
Selvedge denim has closed, non-fraying edges made with white yarn, often with a contrasting yarn that forms a vertical line along the selvedge. It is often manufactured on old-style shuttle narrow looms, resulting in a denim fabric that is usually around 75–85 cm wide (30–35").

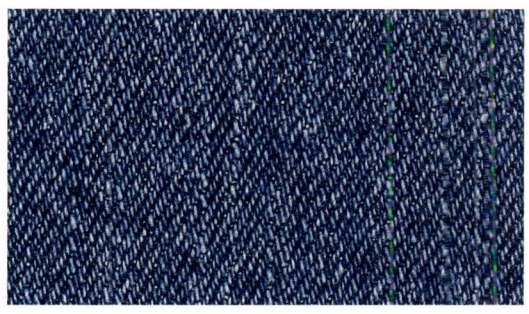

STONEWASHED DENIM
Stonewashed denim has a worn, faded appearance that mimics the look of a pair of well-worn jeans. The name stems from the pumice stones used to achieve this look, but today a similar effect can be done with enzymes.

ENZYME WASH DENIM
A protein-like substance is used to soften and finish denim, creating a stonewashed, worn-out look, but in a more eco-friendly way than traditional stone washing.

ROPING
The wavy diagonal pattern along the leg opening that resembles a rope. Often artificially created in the factory to mimic the effect of worn and washed denim.

WHISKERS
Horizontal crease lines on the front hip area that are artificially created in the denim factory using tools such as sandpaper and even laser in order to replicate the look of naturally aged jeans.

HEMP DENIM
Hemp requires less water and fewer pesticides compared with cotton, so for a more eco-friendly choice, there are now hemp/cotton mix denim fabrics available. Hemp is stiffer, has a coarse surface and shrinks more than cotton, which is why a 100% hemp denim is not an ideal option.

BULL DENIM
Bull denim refers to a heavyweight twill weave, but unlike regular denim, the weft and warp yarns in bull twill have the same colour, creating a uniform weave without the white lines.

CHAMBRAY
Just like denim, chambray has a coloured warp and a white weft. The difference is that chambray warp and weft threads alternate in a 1X1 pattern, whereas denim's warp thread will go over two or three weft threads.

OTHER DENIM COLOURS
Jeans can be made from many different coloured warp yarns, such as red, black and brown. Traditional denim still has white weft yarns running crosswise, regardless of the colour of the warp.

QUICK GUIDE: PICK THE RIGHT DENIM

VINTAGE STYLE JEANS
Pick a dark blue unwashed denim, preferably selvedge denim. Weight: 12–16 oz. Heavier denim than that might be hard to sew on a domestic sewing machine and also have a very stiff hand.

SKINNY JEANS
Use a denim fabric with added Lycra that has at least 20% crosswise stretch, and for super skinny stovepipe jeans, even more stretch might be required. Check the pattern instructions for fabric recommendations. Weight: 9–12 oz depending on style, but beware that lighter denim might show unwanted bulges.

WIDE-LEGGED JEANS
Opt for softer denim with a nice drape and shape. Weight: 9–13 oz.

STRAIGHT-LEGGED, BOYFRIEND AND BOOTCUT JEANS
Cotton, hemp/cotton or Tencel/cotton mix are all suitable for these styles. For more ease of movement, use a fabric that has 1–2% Lycra (Elastane). Weight: 12–14 oz.

FLARED JEANS
Pick a fabric that isn't too stiff. For flared jeans that are fitted around the hip area, use a fabric that has 1–2% Lycra for more comfort and shape. Weight: 10–13 oz.

JEGGINGS
Jeggings (pull-on jeans) usually refers to leggings made to look like denim jeans but sewn with a stretchy knit fabric. Use a denim-look cotton/poly/Lycra knit with medium thickness to sew jeggings.

CARING FOR DENIM FABRIC

SHOULD YOU PRE-WASH THE FABRIC BEFORE CUTTING?

It depends on what you want to achieve. Raw, unwashed denim will generally both shrink and bleed dye that could potentially stain things. From that point of view it makes sense to pre-wash the fabric at least once, but beware that the denim will likely keep bleeding and also shrink a bit more during consecutive washes.

On the other hand, those aiming for a naturally aged and gradually faded look, should avoid pre-washing and wear the jeans for a considerable period of time before washing them. In fact, some jeans aficionados like to wait several months before immersing the jeans into water for the first time.

FACTOR IN SHRINKAGE

Unless the denim has been through a very thorough washing regime in the factory, such as enzyme or stonewashing, the fabric will shrink. Unwashed, raw denim can shrink up to 10% lengthwise (and much less crosswise). As a rule of thumb, expect most denim fabrics to shrink at least 2–5% lengthwise, depending on the weave and pre-treatment.

To test shrinkage, cut a square swatch that is at least 10X10 cm (4X4") and wash it using your planned method. Compare the washed swatch with the original measurements, making sure you get the vertical and horizontal position right. Refer to page 10 to see how the denim warp and weft should run.

Don't cut the swatch along the edge of the fabric because fraying during washing can reduce the size of the swatch even further. Since denim fabric will primarily shrink lengthwise, and any crosswise shrinkage usually stretches back when the jeans are worn, you usually only need to add length to a pattern when using unwashed denim.

HOW TO WASH YOUR JEANS

Hand washing

Warmer water will remove more of the denim dye than colder water and also make the fabric shrink more. Hand washing will be more gentle than machine washing, so wash your precious denim with soap in a bathtub or sink using lukewarm water; just make sure the indigo colour doesn't bond with the enamel. Another option is to use the kitchen sink if it's made of metal.

Machine washing

Turn your jeans inside out, close the zipper and fasten the buttons. Washing the jeans inside out will preserve the colour better, and closing the metal hardware helps to avoid additional wears and tears. When washing dark denim, don't mix the jeans with other types of garments because the indigo colour from the jeans will most likely stain them.

Wash the jeans in lukewarm water, 35–40°C (95–10°F) on a short, delicate cycle. For darker denim, use a detergent that preserves colours.

DRYING

A tumble dryer will wear down denim fabric quicker. To prevent at least some of this, tumble dry on a delicate cycle with a low heat setting and remove the jeans before they are completely dry. Then hang the jeans straight and let them air dry.

You also have to be careful with the dryer when washing stretch denim because the heat and agitation can damage the Lycra (Elastane), causing the threads to break down and the fabric to ultimately lose its stretch.

To preserve the fabric even more, avoid the tumble dryer altogether and let the jeans air dry, without any added heat.

RESTORING FADED DENIM

There are special back-to-blue dyes that can restore faded denim, but be aware that they will also add some colour to the white weft threads that are part of the denim fabric signature look.

DENIM AND SUSTAINABILITY

5 REASONS WHY DENIM JEANS ARE PROBLEMATIC

1. Denim drains our water resources. It takes around 10,000 litres (approximately 2,600 gallons) of water to produce the 700 grams (1.5 pounds) of cotton required to make one pair of jeans, according to the World Wildlife Fund. This can lead to a shortage of precious freshwater.

2. The dyes and washes pollute the water. If the wastewater is dumped straight into waterways the result can be very harmful to both humans and the wildlife. Often filled with dangerous chemicals, metals and dark blue colour, the polluted water can no longer be used for consumption and cleaning. The chemicals can cause skin blisters, and some studies have concluded that some denim dyes may be linked to an increased risk of cancer (Singh & Chadha, 'Textile Industry and Occupational Cancer', 2016).

3. Distressed denim can be a hazard to factory workers. Sandblasting, polishing, chemical spraying and dye-application are popular methods for distressing jeans. However, these methods can cause many health issues among factory workers.

4. Poor working conditions. Most denim fabrics and garments are produced in countries where a majority of workers have very low wages and long working hours. Poor safety conditions, exposure to dangerous chemicals and dust and a lack of worker's rights are also still prevalent in many textile factories around the world.

5. The hardware on jeans makes them harder to recycle. Rivets, zippers, buttons, patches and labels have to be removed before the jeans can be sent to shredding to be recycled.

DENIM AND SUSTAINABILITY

5 WAYS TO MAKE JEANS MORE SUSTAINABLE

1. Make jeans that are built to last. Opt for good quality fabric and notions, make sure the jeans fit before you cut the fabric, use good craftsmanship, take good care of your handmade jeans and mend them when needed.

2. Choose a hemp or Tencel denim blend. Preferably a fabric blend mixed with organic or recycled cotton. Hemp and Tencel require less energy, water and dangerous chemicals compared with conventionally grown cotton.

3. Say no to harmful chemicals. Avoid fabrics that have been treated with hazardous bleaches to create a worn, washed look.

4. Keep metal hardware to a minimum. Use bar tacks instead of rivets and metal sew-on buttons rather than shank buttons because the former are easier to remove if the jeans need to be discarded.

5. Buy certified denim fabric. Check for the Fair Trade certification by the WFTO to assure better working conditions and official eco-certifications for more environmentally friendly production methods.

CUTTING DENIM

PRE-SHRINKING
Untreated denim fabric will shrink, especially lengthwise and can sometimes shrink even more after the first wash. Either pre-wash the fabric or adjust the pattern so that it has extra allowance for shrinkage. For more detailed information on pre-washing denim, see *Caring for denim* on page 16.

PRE-PRESSING
If the denim is wrinkly after washing and storage, iron it out first before cutting it.

CUTTING DIRECTION
Regular twill-weave denim can be cut in both directions, which means that you can rotate the pattern pieces 180 degrees to save fabric. If you are using napped fabric, such as corduroy or velvet, all pieces must be cut in the same direction because the colour and sheen will look different depending on the direction. For raw, untreated denim; use a single layer layout with the same pieces next to each other (but in opposite direction) to prevent the seams from twisting.

FOLDED OR SINGLE-LAYER CUTTING LAYOUT
When working with wider denim fabrics, you can cut the fabric on the fold to save space and time. But denim woven on a narrow loom might require cutting all the pieces separately on a single layer, especially if you are sewing jeans that use the selvedge as the outer edge (layout B). If the denim is very thick, it's also better to cut one piece at the time as a single layer.

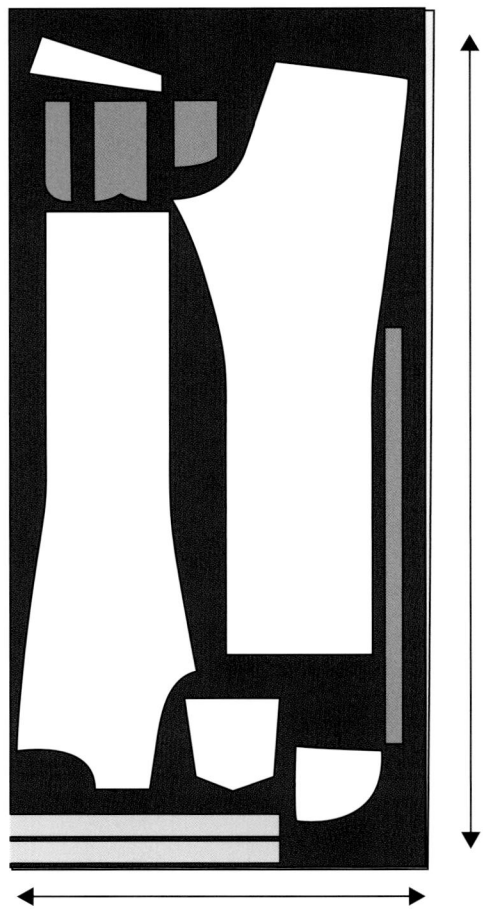

A. Folded cutting layout

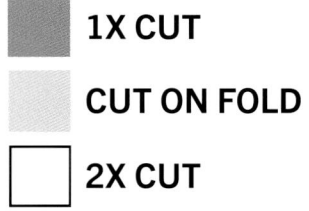

STRAIGHTENING THE ENDS

To ensure that the grain aligns when cutting on folded fabrics, straighten the crosswise ends. Place a wide ruler along the selvedge and cut the fabric at a 90-degree angle, horizontally.

FOLDING THE FABRIC FOR CUTTING

Align the torn crosswise edge and the selvedge. Smooth out the fabric to make sure there are no wrinkles or bumps.

NOTCHES

Use your preferred method to mark the notches on the fabric (e.g., cutting snips, tracing chalk or thread-marking). The quickest way is to cut tiny snips into the seam allowance using a pair of very sharp shears. Keep in mind that those snips can become hard to see once the edges are overcast. In those cases, use a little chalk, too, for extra visibility.

RIGHT OR REVERSE SIDE

Jeans can be cut from either the right or reverse side. However, cutting from the right side generally makes markings easier because white chalk is more visible on darker denim.

PLACING THE PATTERN PIECES

Measure the distance from the selvedge to the grainline arrows, making sure there is equal distance from the top to the bottom of the arrow on each pattern piece. To keep the fabric in place, pattern weights are generally better than pins because pins can distort the fabric somewhat, and on tightly woven, heavy denim, they can also be hard to insert properly.

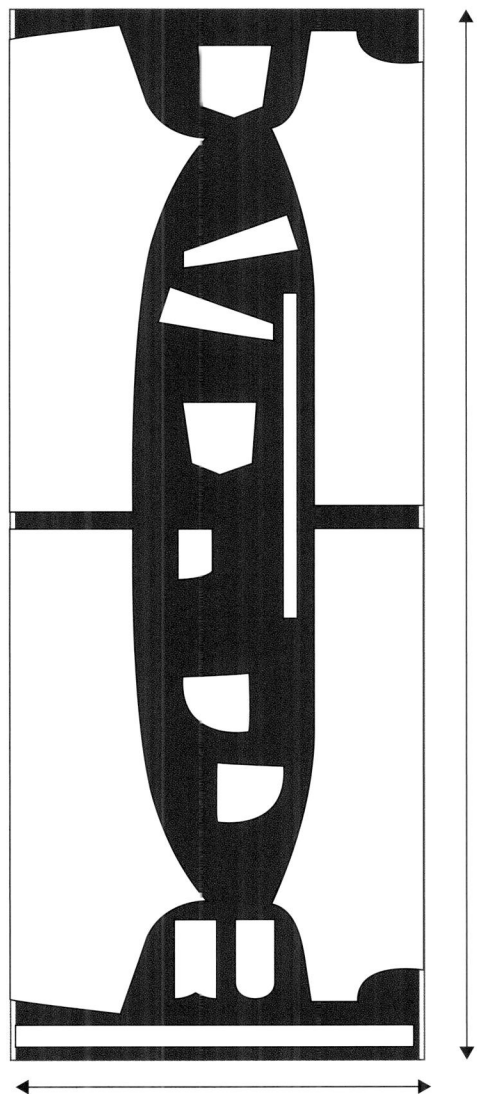

B. Selvedge, single layer cutting layout

CUTTING TOOLS

Use a rotary cutter with a mat or very sharp tailor's sheers to cut denim fabric.

CUTTING DENIM 21

CHAPTER 2
PATTERNS

JEANS PATTERN PIECES

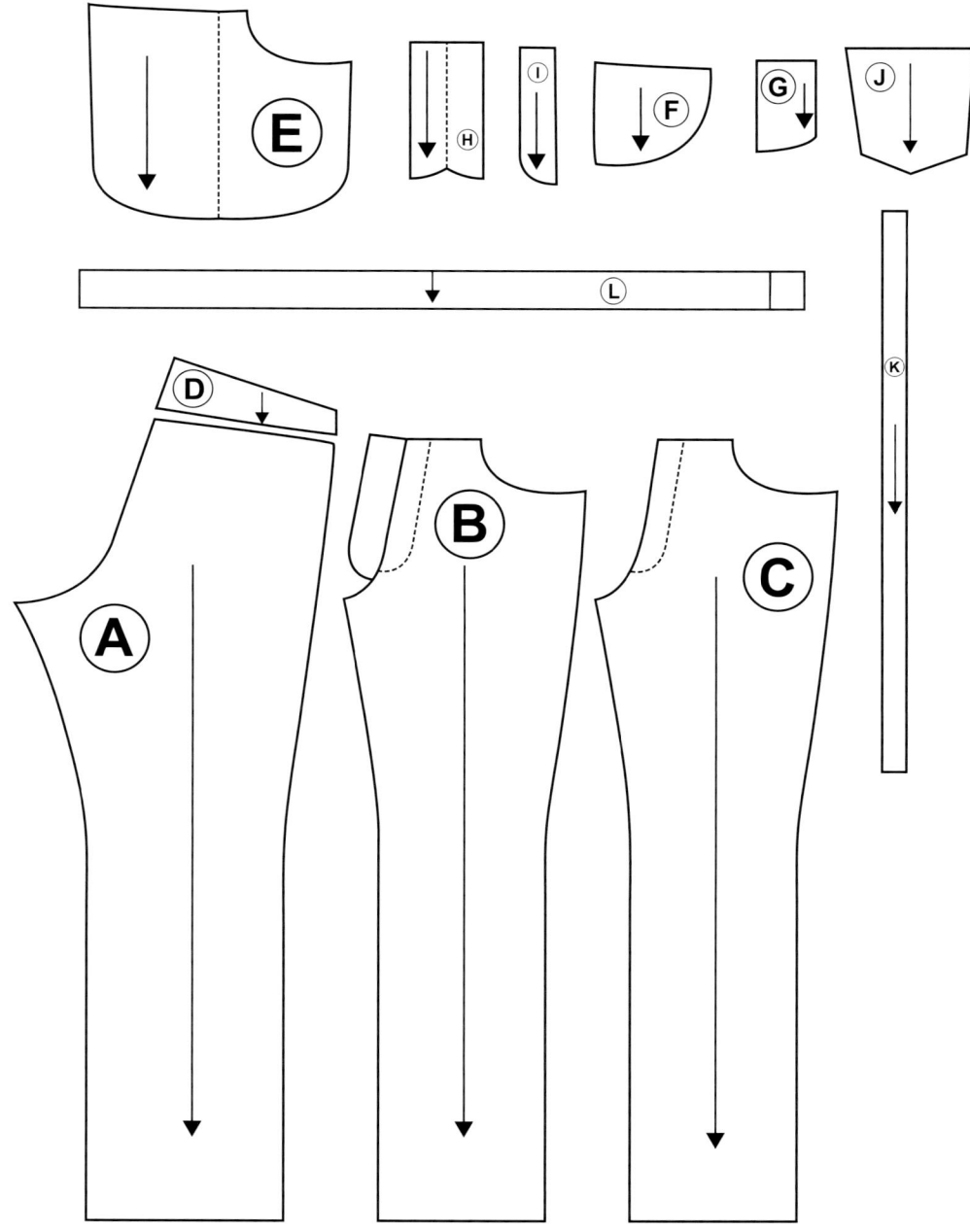

A. Back piece
B. Front piece with facing
C. Front piece without facing
D. Yoke
E. Front pocket lining
F. Pocket shield (backing)
G. Coin pocket
H. Fly shield (backing)
I. Fly facing
J. Back pocket
K. Belt loop piece
L. Waistband

A GUIDE TO SEAM ALLOWANCES

Using the proper seam allowances makes sewing easier and more precise. The allowances suggested in this guide are based on garment industry practises but can of course be changed, depending on the project and your preferred sewing method.

Side seams, yoke and crotch (overlocked)
12 mm (½")

Flat-felled seams
12 mm (½") to 25 mm (1") depending on method used

Hem allowance (folded twice)
30 mm (1¼")

Waistband (L)
10–12 mm (⅜–½") on all sides

Back pocket (J)
Top opening (folded twice)
25 mm (1")
Sides and lower edge (folded once)
12 mm (½")

Front piece pocket opening (B & C)
8 mm (⅓")

Front pocket lining (E)
Pocket opening
8 mm (⅓")
Pocket lining side seam
12 mm (½")
Pocket lining lower edge
20 mm (¾") French seam
12 mm (½") overlocked

Front pocket backing (F)
Top (enclosed in the waistband)
10–12 mm (⅜–½")
Side seam
12 mm (½")
Lower edge
None if overlocked
8 mm (⅓") if folded

Center front (zipper and button fly)
Left center front piece (C)
12 mm (½")
Right center front piece (B)
12 mm (½"), and if the pattern lacks the extension, add 6 mm (¼") extra on along the fly area for the fly shield

Key pocket (G)
Top opening (folded twice)
25 mm (1")
Sides (folded once)
12 mm (½")
Lower edge
None if only overlocked
12 mm (½") if folded

Fly shield (H)
Side seam
12 mm (½")
Top (enclosed in the waistband)
10–12 mm (⅜–½")
Lower edge
12 mm (½") if folded
None if only overlocked

Fly facing (I)
Center front seam
12 mm (½")
Top edge (enclosed in the waistband)
10–12 mm (⅜–½")
Lower edge
None if the edge is left unfolded and overlocked

JEANS STYLE PATTERN CHANGES

SELVEDGE CUT JEANS

On selvedge jeans the outseam is cut along the decorative selvedge of the denim fabric. This means that the outseam needs to be straight, which requires some pattern changes.

Normally a pair of selvedge jeans is worn turned-up, so add extra length to accommodate for the fold or folds. A standard fold for selvedge jeans is a single fold around 5 cm (2") long.

1. Straighten the outseams. Draw vertical lines from the top of the front and back pieces.

2. Reduce inseam width on the front piece. Start at crotch point or slightly below and taper in so that the width at knee level is approximately the same as the original.

3. Trim crotch on the back piece. Remove around 20 mm (¾") at the crotch tip. Scope out the crotch so that crotch length stays approximately the same as on the original pattern piece.

4. Reduce inseam on the back piece. Start at the redrafted crotch and taper in so that the width at knee level remains approximately the same as the original pattern piece.

5. Extend the leg length. Add around 5 cm (2") to the length for a single fold or more length for a double fold.

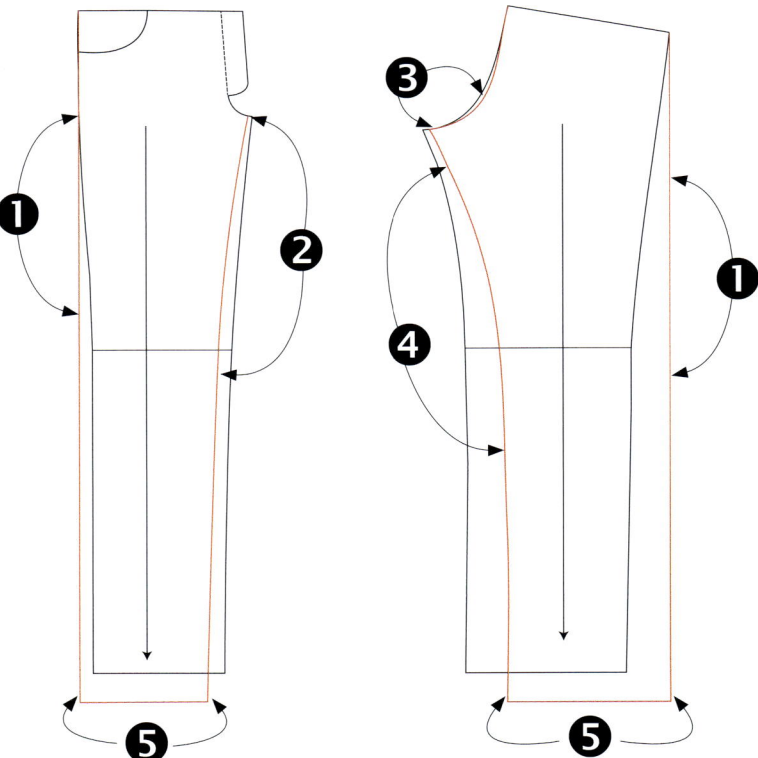

SKINNY JEANS

These adjustments are used for turning a straight leg non-stretch jeans pattern into a pair of skinny jeans using stretch denim.

The measurements given are just suggestions and will depend on factors such as the original pattern, fabric choice and personal preferences.

1. **Remove around 5 mm (¼") of the waist-width on the front piece.** Curve out at hip level.

2. **Remove around 5 mm (¼") at the mid-back crotch.**

3. **Scope out crotch curve around 15–20 mm (⅝–¾").**

4. **Remove width on yoke mid-back.** Reduce the same amount as the crotch mid-back (2) on the yoke.

5. **Remove the sum of 1 and 2 at the mid-back on the waistband.** Here 10 mm in total.

6. **Reduce back inseam.** Trim around 15 mm (⅜") at the crotch, shape towards a 20 mm (¾") reduction at the knee.

7. **Reduce front inseam.** Trim around 10 mm (⅜") at crotch and shape towards a 20 mm (¾") reduction at knee.

8. **Reduce front outseam.** Start at thigh level, shape towards a 20 mm (¾") reduction at the knee.

9. **Reduce back outseam.** Beginning at outer thigh level, shape towards a 20 mm (¾") reduction at the knee.

10. **Narrow down and shorten the hem.** Remove between 20–25 mm (¾–1") on all sides and shorten the leg 5 cm (2").

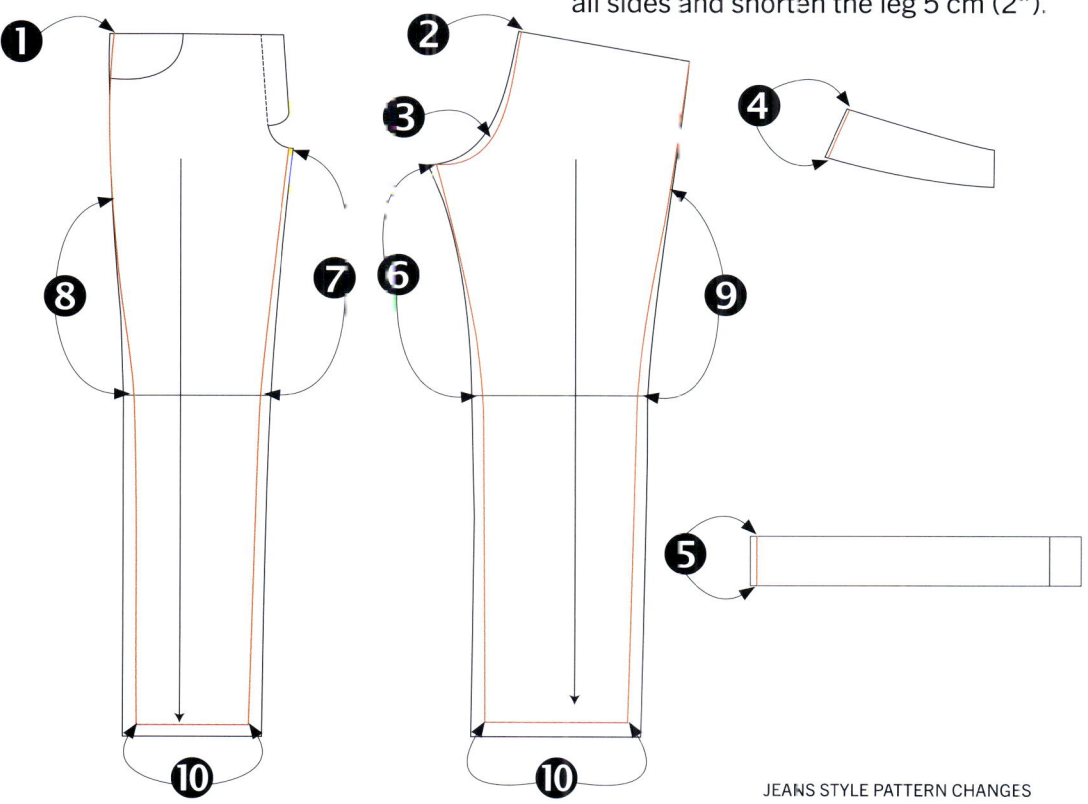

JEANS STYLE PATTERN CHANGES

FLARED JEANS

Also called bell-bottoms, flared jeans have a very wide leg opening. This effect is created by adding width to both the inseams and outseams. This style generally has a relaxed fit around the hip and thigh area, unlike bootcut jeans, which tend to be more fitted.

1. **Add width to the front and back outseam.** Start at the upper hip, flare out the seam gradually. The flare angle should increase from the knee for a more pronounced look. Depending on the original leg opening, add at least 5 cm (2") at the hem on the outseam.

2. **Add width to the back inseam.** Start at the crotch, flare out the inseam using a gently curved line.

3. **Extend the flare more at knee level.** Starting from knee height, flare out to add the same extra width as you did on the outseams (here 5 cm/2").

4. **Add width to the front inseam.** Start at the crotch, flare out the inseam gradually. At knee height, increase the flare more by slanting the line outwards to add the total of 5 cm (2") in this example.

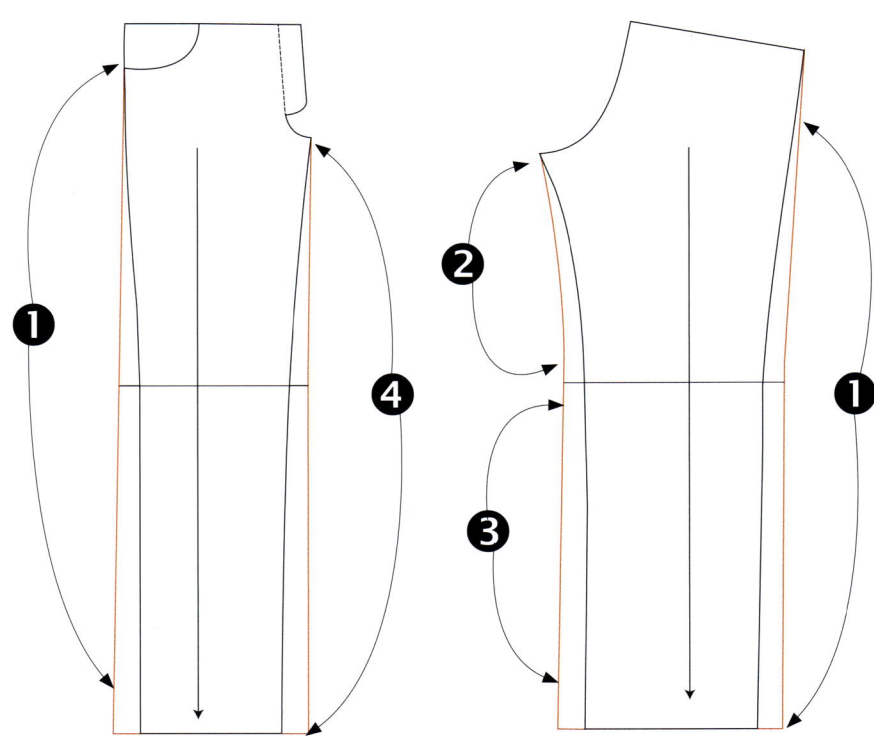

BOOTCUT JEANS

Bootcut jeans are tapered at the knee with a subtle flare towards the leg opening.

1. **Taper in the front outseam.** Start at crotch level, taper in the leg width to around 12–20 mm (½–¾") at knee.

2. **Taper in the back outseam.** Start at crotch level, taper in leg width to around 12–20 mm (½–¾") at the knee.

3. **Taper front inseam.** Start at crotch level, taper in leg width to around 12–20 mm (½–¾") at knee level.

4. **Taper back inseam.** Start at crotch level, taper in leg width to around 12–20 mm (½–¾") at knee.

5. **Increase leg opening around 20 mm (¾") on all sides.** Start at knee level, shape out the seams towards the hem.

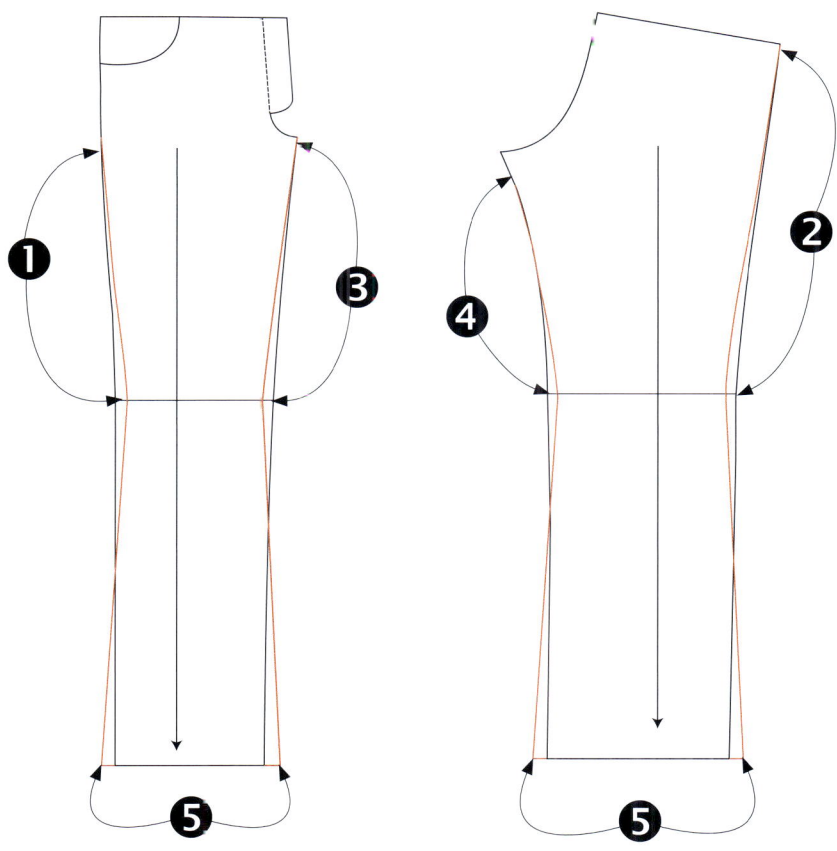

DRAFTING A CURVED WAISTBAND

A curved waistband is cut slightly on the bias with a tapered fit on top, which can prevent gaping and is more comfortable to wear because the bias cut allows for more stretch, even on 100% cotton jeans. The method shown here is ideal if you want to turn a rectangular waistband into one with a gentle curve. For an even more contoured waistband, splice and overlap the waistband at more locations than shown in this tutorial.

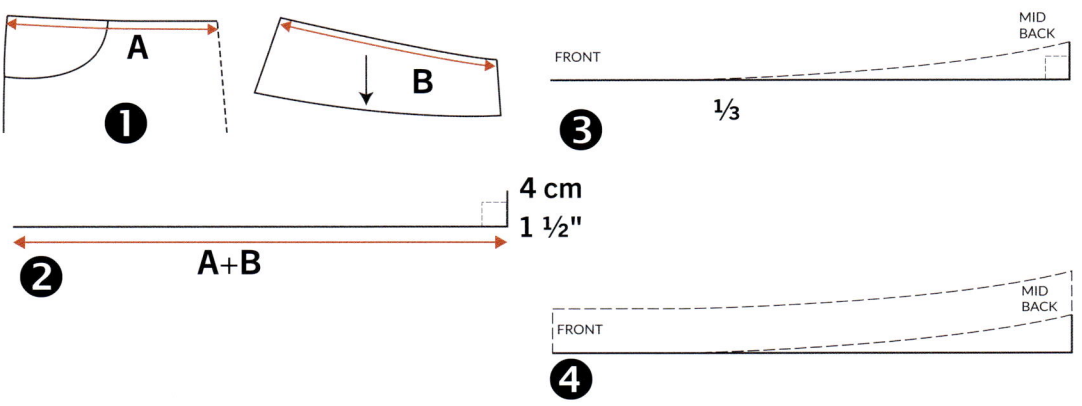

1. Measure the waist. Measure the length of the upper edge of the yoke and front piece (excluding the seam allowances). This measurement corresponds to half of the total waist circumference. Or measure the distance of the rectangular waistband, without seam allowances and fly extension, to get the same information.

2. Using tracing paper, draw perpendicular lines. The horizontal line should be the same as the waist measurement taken in step 1 (half of the total waist circumference). The vertical line should be approximately 4 cm (1½") long.

3. Shape the waistband. Around one-third in, curve the waistband upwards to the tip of the vertical line. Measure the curved line to make sure it has the same length as the waist circumference. If needed, add or remove extra length mid-front (the straight area).

4. Draw a second parallel line. The space between the lines should be the same width as the finished waistband (without seam allowances). Between 3.5–5 cm (1⅜–2") is a good width for a curved jeans waistband using this pattern drafting method. Cut out the drafted waistband from the paper.

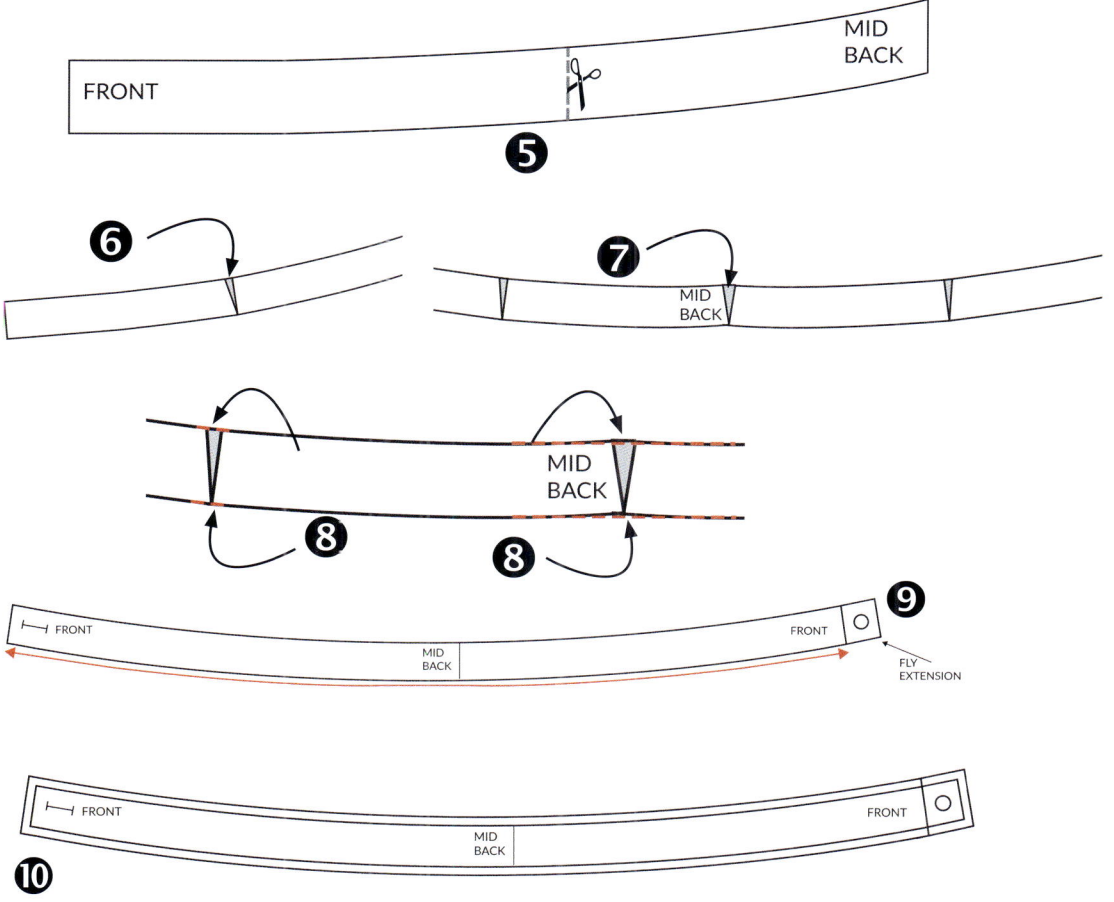

5. Cut open a vertical line on the waistband. Place the cut approximately in the middle of the pattern piece.

6. Overlap to reduce length. Start with the side; remove length at the top by tilting the split pieces so that they overlap. Tape together.

7. Duplicate and overlap the two waistband pieces at mid-back to remove more length. Check the top waist measure on the body to ensure a good fit on the body. Tape together.

8. Smooth out all the curves. Then add a vertical grain line mid-back. Retrace the pattern after you have done the changes.

9. Add a fly extension on the left-hand side of the waistband. If you are adapting a finished pattern with a straight waistband, add the same width here as on the original waistband. Otherwise, add around 4 cm (1½") to the extension. Mark the button and buttonhole.

10. Add seam allowances. Add approximately 10 mm (⅜") seam allowances on all sides.

HOW TO FIX COMMON JEANS FITTING ISSUES

This guide shows how you can alter the pattern to solve common jeans fitting issues. Because pants fitting is a complex topic that is worthy of an entire book in itself, check out the list of fitting books on page 186 for more resources on the topic.

SMILE LINES

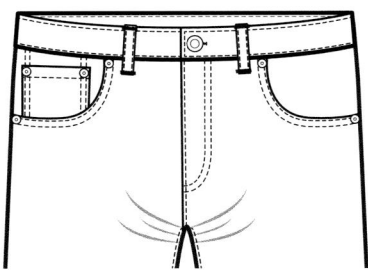

ISSUE: The fabric pulls around the thigh area, creating horizontal or diagonal drag lines (smiles) around the crotch area. This means there is too little room around the crotch and upper thigh area.

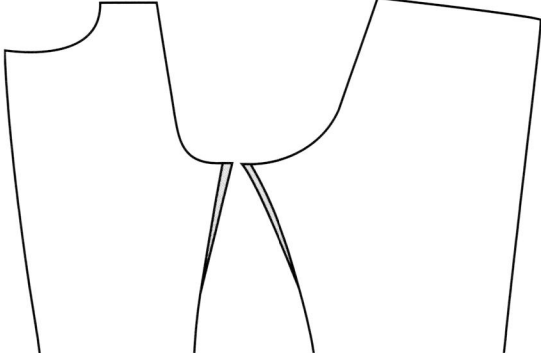

SOLUTION: Add width to the inseam on the front and/or back piece, depending on where the smile lines occur. This will extend the crotch seam and add more room for the thighs.

WRINKLES ACROSS LOWER HIP

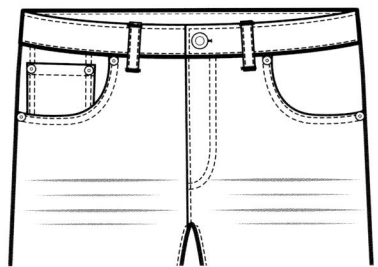

ISSUE: The pants are too tight. Mostly seen in the front area around the lower hip, just above the thighs.

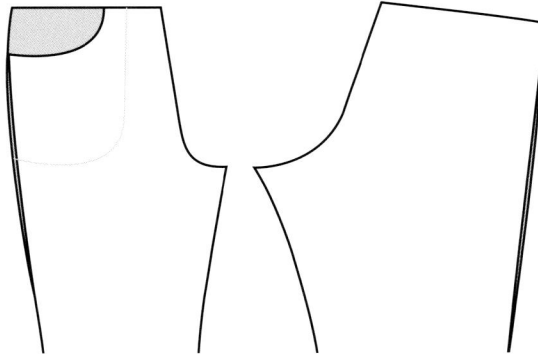

SOLUTION: Add more width to the outseams on both the front and back pieces. Note that on super skinny stretch jeans, it's hard to eliminate this istsue completely because the jeans are supposed to fit tightly around this area.

PULL LINES ACROSS BACK HIP

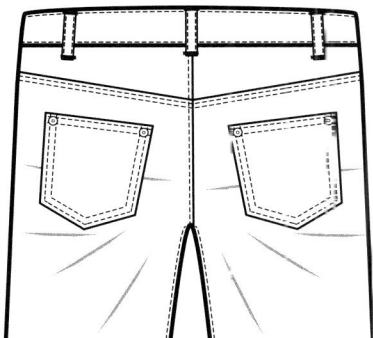

ISSUE: Wrinkles across the back hip area. The jeans feel uncomfortable when sitting and might ride down. The back crotch is too short and there is not enough width around the hip area. Common on those with a fuller derrière.

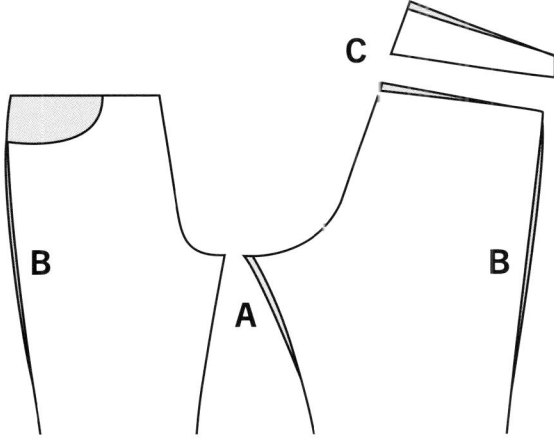

SOLUTION: This issue is usually fixed with several, smaller changes rather than one single fix.

A. Add width to the inseam on the back piece. This will extend the crotch seam and add more room for the hips and upper thighs.

B. Add more width to the outseams around the hip area.

C. If needed, also extend the top of the mid-back crotch to add even more length to the crotch. You can do this either on the back piece or the yoke, or ideally a combination of both.

WRINKLES BELOW HIP

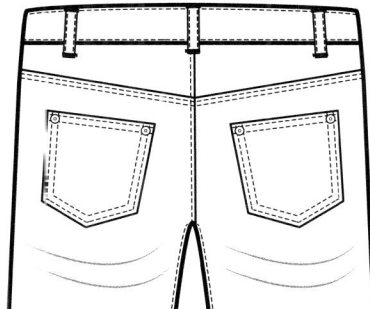

ISSUE: Excess fabric drops down, creating horizontal or diagonal folds along the upper back thighs. This is caused by a flatter bum that doesn't fill out the entire back area.

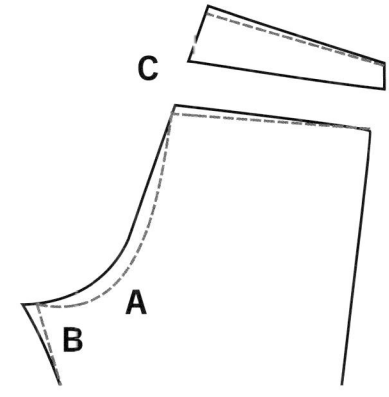

SOLUTION: Start by removing excess fabric by deepening the crotch curve (**A**). If needed, also take in the inseam to shorten the crotch length (**B**). Another option is to lower the mid-back waist on the yoke and/or back piece, which also shortens the crotch length (**C**).

WRINKLES ACROSS TUMMY

ISSUE: Horizontal or diagonal wrinkles across the tummy and front upper hip, which means that the jeans are too tight around the tummy area.

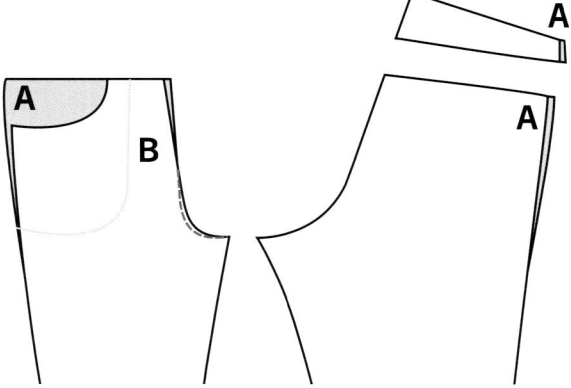

SOLUTION: Use a combination of adding more width to the outseams (**A**) and front crotch plus straightening a slanted front crotch seam (**B**). Remember to extend the waistband if you make the top of the jeans wider.

SWAY BACK

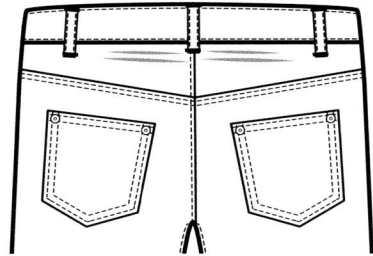

ISSUE: The jeans sag and gape in the back, forming horizontal wrinkles mid-back. This is because the upper back of the jeans is not filled up due to a sway back.

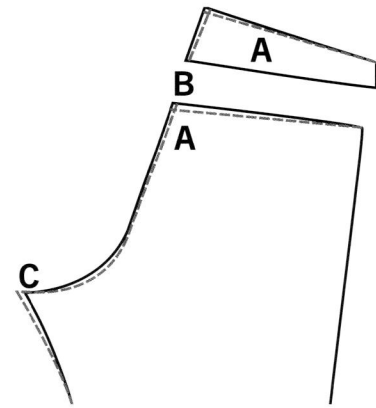

SOLUTION: This issue often requires a combination of fixes. Start by lowering the back waistline slightly on either the yoke, the back piece or a combination of both (**A**).

If there is also gaping in the back, take in the mid-back crotch seam slightly on both the yoke and back piece (**B**). For more adjustments see the Gaping back section on page.

To prevent the jeans from riding down due to a shortened back crotch, extend the back crotch length slightly (**C**).

VERTICAL LINES ALONG THIGHS

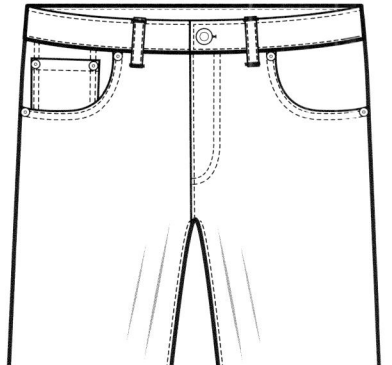

ISSUE: Vertical folds along the inner leg. This is caused by too much fabric around the inseam of the jeans.

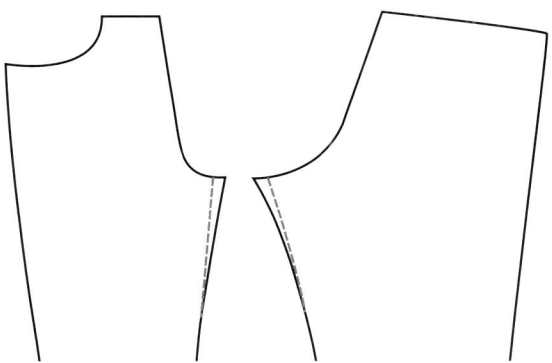

SOLUTION: Take in the inseam to shorten the crotch length. Do this on the front or back piece or both, depending on where the wrinkles occur.

VERTICAL FOLDS AT CROTCH

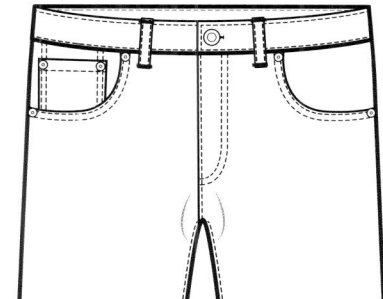

ISSUE: Excess fabric creates curved, vertical folds around the front crotch area, just above the thighs.

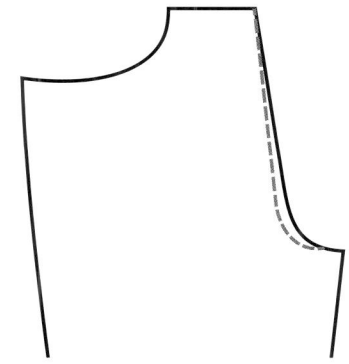

SOLUTION: The front crotch curve needs to be deeper. Scope out the crotch until the fabric folds disappear. Straightening the crotch seam can also help solve this fitting issue.

SHORTEN AND LENGTHEN JEANS

SHORTEN: Fold the pattern where you need to shorten the length (e.g., above the knee). Insert paper underneath and shape new side seams.

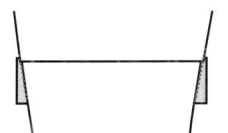

LENGTHEN: Cut open the pattern where you need extra length (e.g., below the knee). Insert paper to fill the gap and shape the new seams.

GAPING BACK

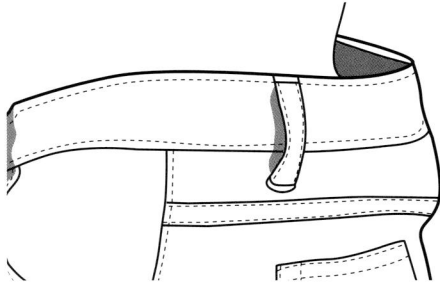

ISSUE: The jeans gapes in the back, which is caused by too much width in the upper back of the jeans.

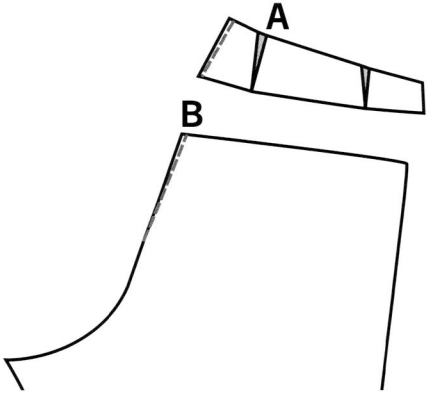

SOLUTION: Remove excess width at the back by doing the following:

Splice the yoke at two spots and overlap the pieces to make the upper edge narrower (**A**). If that is not enough, take in the back crotch seam, starting at the back piece and tapering gradually on the yoke (**B**).

A curved waistband rather than a rectangular one can also help with this issue. See *Drafting a curved waistband* on page 30 for instructions on how to construct a shaped waistband.

TIGHTNESS AROUND THE CALVES

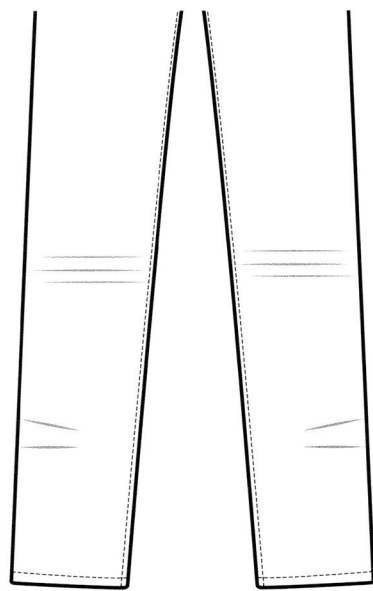

ISSUE: The jeans fit snugly over the calves, with the side seams pulling back and causing the jeans to ride up with wrinkles around the knee area

SOLUTION: Starting just above the knee, add more width by gradually shaping the inseam and outseam of the back piece.

IMPORTANT NOTES ABOUT FITTING

- Due to the assembly process (see page 68 and onwards), it's hard to fit jeans as you sew. Instead, it's better to do the alterations on a test garment using a fabric that has similar properties to the denim you plan to use. Another option is to use a pattern drafted on tissue paper and do the pattern alterations on the body.

- Like the fit of a pair of jeans that you already own? Use that pair as your starting point, checking for key measurements such as hip, thigh and waist width, crotch length and ease.

- Remember that certain alterations can cause other fit issues. For instance, if you shorten the crotch to remove excess fabric, you might end up with a crotch that rides down when you sit. This is why it's often good to combine a few smaller alterations, rather than adjusting just one area.

- Because the back is made of two pieces, the yoke and the back leg piece, you might need to alter both pattern pieces in order to get a balanced fit.

- When adding width to the front outseam, you also need to add the same amount to the pocket lining and shield. Also remember that the outer top part of the front piece consists of just the pocket lining and shield and not the actual front piece.

- Always check the length of the altered inseams and outseams so that the seams of the back and front pieces still are equal in length. The upper curve on the inner back seam should, however, be slightly shorter than the corresponding front inseam and then stretched out while sewn.

- If altering the shape of the yoke and the upper parts of the back piece, again check that the measurements are still corresponding.

- When adjusting the width around the waist, remember to also alter the waistband pattern piece.

- Don't obsess over getting rid of every little wrinkle if that leads to more uncomfortable jeans. Also, denim fabric will shape and stretch out when worn, so don't expect your jeans to fit the same way every day.

CHAPTER 3
TOOLS & NOTIONS

SEWING MACHINE EQUIPMENT

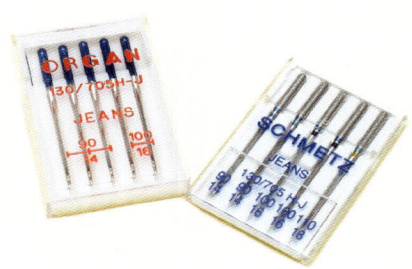

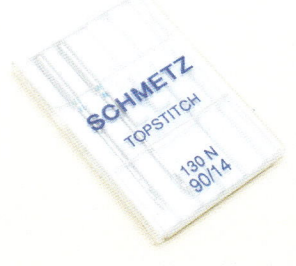

DENIM SEWING MACHINE NEEDLES
Reinforced needles designed to sew through thick fabrics without breaking. Come in many sizes. A good range to have in the sew kit is 90/14, 100/16 and 110/18, depending on the denim used.

TOPSTITCH NEEDLES
Topstitch needles have an extra-large eye with room for thick threads, making them a good choice for topstitching denim. Use size 90/14 or 100/16 depending on the thickness of the fabric.

DENIM TWIN-NEEDLE
A double needle designed to be used when sewing denim and other thick fabrics. Can be used for topstitching and sewing belt loops on a sewing machine.

STANDARD PRESSER FOOT
The standard presser foot can be used for most jeans seams, even buttonholes when sewn freehand.

EDGE STITCH PRESSER FOOT

A presser foot with a guide blade that makes it very easy to topstitch evenly along edges and seams.

BUTTONHOLE PRESSER FOOT

A manual buttonhole foot is often a better choice for jeans because automatic feet can have problems feeding properly over thick layers. The slot in the middle makes gauging the placement of the rows easier.

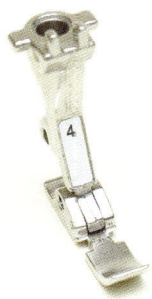

JEANS PRESSER FOOT

Some sewing machine brands also have a dedicated topstitch/jeans presser foot designed especially for sewing straight stitches over thick layers of fabric.

ZIPPER PRESSER FOOT

Narrow presser foot that allows for sewing very close to the zipper teeth. Can also be used for edge stitching and any situation where the space is too small for a regular presser foot.

FLAT-FELLING PRESSER FOOT
A presser foot constructed to fell a seam using a two-step process. Most sewing machine brands have a version of this foot.

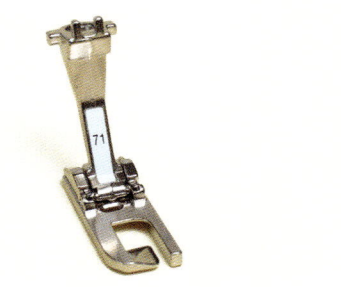

BELT LOOP FOLDER
An attachment that can be used both on a coverstitch and a sewing machine. The folder is placed in front of the presser foot and folds the belt loop strips evenly.

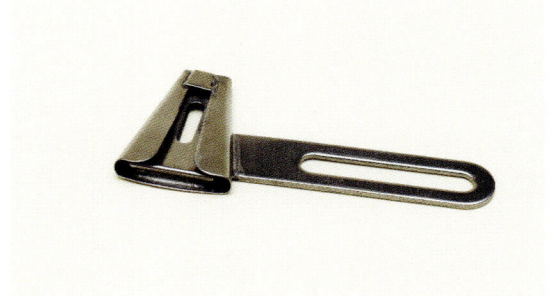

BIAS TAPE FOLDER
Can be used both to create belt loops and as an attachment to fold the strips while sewing. For the latter to work you might need an extension table or a plate to give the bias tape folder enough space.

HUMP-JUMPER
A tool that keeps the presser foot horizontal when sewing over bulky layers and edges. Prevents skipped stitches and helps with even feeding. Also called jean-a-ma-jig or bulky seam aid.

HANDHELD TOOLS

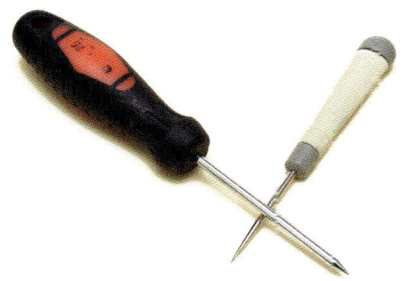

AWL
A sharp tool used for marking, piercing holes for rivets and creating the round opening on keyhole buttonholes. Use the smaller tailor's awl for markings and the larger awl for piercing holes.

BUTTONHOLE CUTTER
A buttonhole cutter makes very clean cuts and is usually a better choice than a seam ripper to open the buttonholes because it is both sharper and more precise. Combine with a round cutter for keyhole buttonholes.

MULTITOOL PLIERS
Pliers with interchangeable tools for attaching jeans buttons and rivets and piercing holes. Note that some sewing brands have pliers that are primarily compatible with their own range of tools and notions.

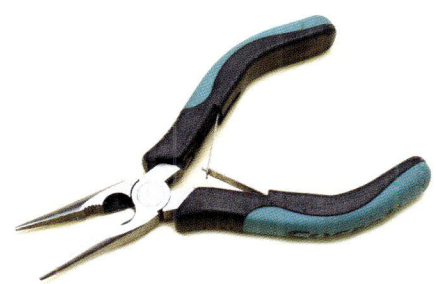

OTHER PLIERS
Needle nose pliers (pictured) are perfect for removing surplus zipper teeth when shortening a zipper. Sharp pliers can be used for shortening nails that are too long when attaching rivets and buttons.

ROTARY CUTTER
Makes cutting straight lines easier, and is especially useful for belt loops, waistbands and back pockets. Use in combination with a cutting mat.

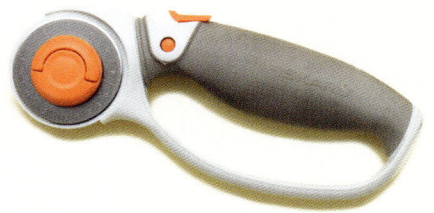

SCISSORS
A pair of sturdy tailor's scissors with sharp blades are the best shears for cutting denim. Scissors can also be used for cutting the marking notches.

HAMMER
For attaching rivets and buttons and hammering down bulky seams to make topstitching easier. A rubber mallet is also a useful tool to have when making jeans.

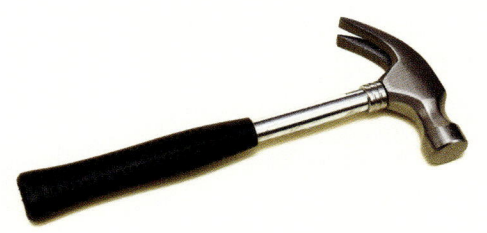

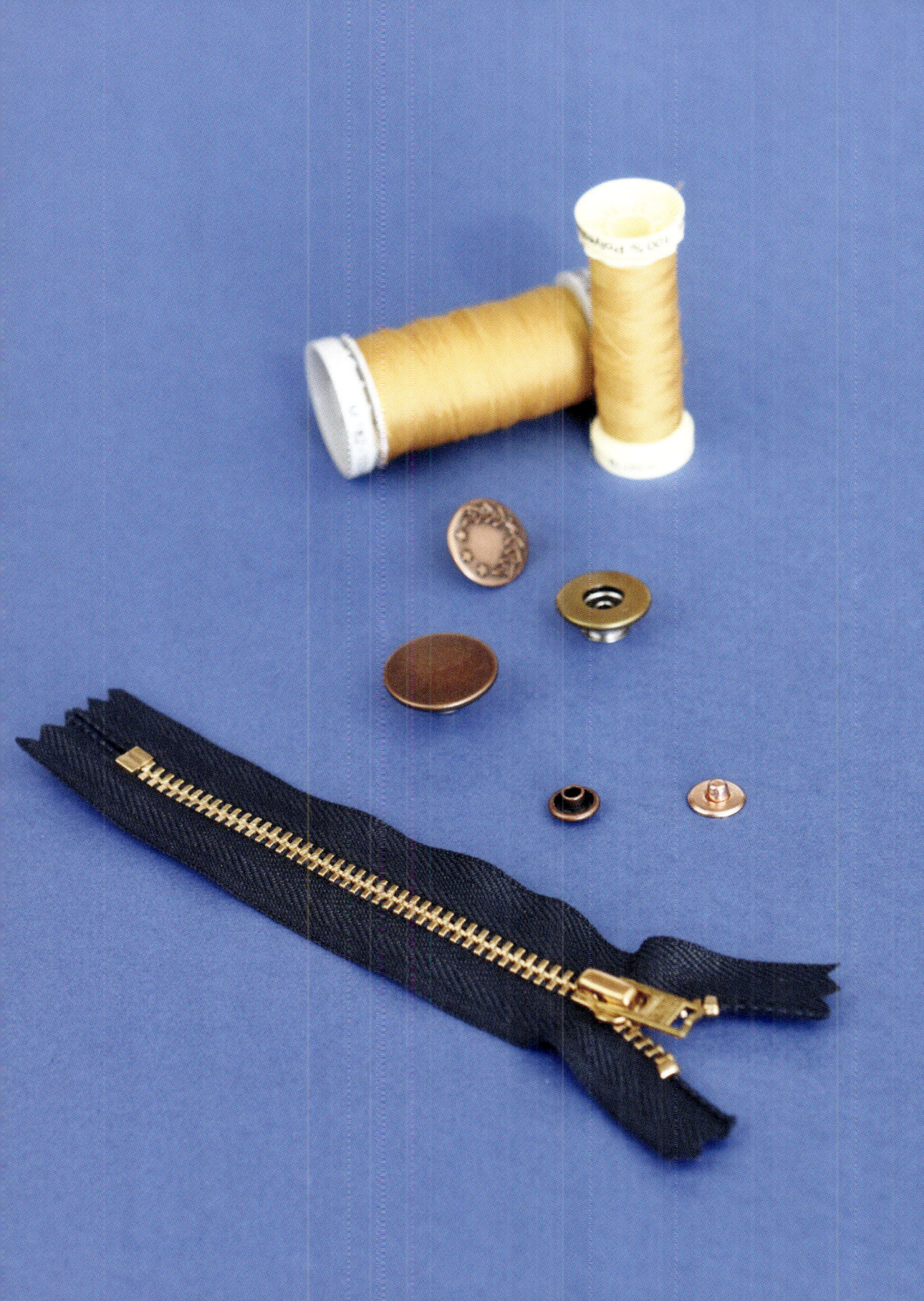

NOTIONS

JEANS/EXTRA STRONG THREAD
Thick durable polyester thread used for topstitching denim. Suitable for denim and topstitching needles sizes 90/14 to 110/18. Heavy buttonhole thread can also be used for topstitching jeans.

REGULAR THREAD
For sewing together the seams on a sewing machine and in the bobbin when topstitching. Two strands of regular sewing machine thread in the needle can substitute heavy thread for topstitching jeans.

SERGER THREAD
Slightly thinner than regular sewing machine thread and a good choice when overcasting the edges on a serger or in the looper on a coverstitch machine.

WOOLLY NYLON
Flossy thread that can be used as a decorative element in the looper when serging the edges and doing chainstitches on a coverstitch machine.

BUTTONS
Jeans buttons come in many different varieties, including flat top, donut shaped, engraved, embossed, enamel and various metals. The button is usually attached with a nail that is inserted from the reverse side.

RIVETS
Used to reinforce high-stress seams such as the pocket areas. Sometimes they are used solely as a decorative feature. Like the buttons, rivets are secured with nails.

JEANS ZIPPER
Closed-end metal zipper. Common metal finishes are golden brass, copper and silver. Always buy a quality zipper that is built to last because replacing a jeans zipper is very cumbersome.

INTERFACING
Use fusible interfacing to stabilise the waistband and jeans fly area. Best suited for denim making are light to mid-weight non-woven or knit fusibles. There is no need for thick interfacing because denim fabric has enough stability by itself. For waistbands on very stretchy jeans, chose a knit fusible interfacing.

CHAPTER 4
SEAMS

QUICK GUIDE: STITCHES FOR JEANS

STITCH	LOOK	USE	PROPERTIES
STRAIGHT STITCH		• Hemming • Topstitching • Bar tacks • Seams	• Durable • Easy to sew • Non-bulky
1-NEEDLE CHAINSTITCH		• Hemming • Topstitching • Basting • Seams	• Not as durable as a straight stitch • Creates the iconic roping effect on hems
2-NEEDLE COVERSTITCH		• Belt loops	• Professional look • Non-bulky • Quick to sew
3-THREAD OVERLOCK		• Overcasting	• Quick to sew • Non-bulky
4-THREAD OVERLOCK		• Overcasting	• Quick to sew • More bulky than the 3-thread overlock • Great coverage

QUICK GUIDE: STITCHES FOR JEANS

STITCH	LOOK	USE	PROPERTIES
ZIGZAG STITCH		• Overcasting • Bar tacks • Decorative stitching	• Durable • Can be hard to sew on thick layers
TWIN-NEEDLE		• Belt loops • Topstitching • Decorative stitching	• Easy to sew • For sewing machines • Stretch seam
TRIPLE STRAIGHT STITCH		• Hemming • Topstitching • Reinforcing seams	• Very durable • Stretch seam • Creates a thick decorative stitch
5-THREAD SAFETY STITCH		• Side seams	• Only available on serger/coverstitch combo machines • Sews seams and finishes them in one go

TIPS FOR TOPSTITCHING

Sewing the highly visible rows of topstitching on denim can feel a bit intimidating, but with the right tools and techniques, you will be able to achieve beautiful stitching on most domestic sewing machines.

HEAVY THREAD

Often called *heavy duty* or *extra strong*, traditional denim topstitching thread is usually made of 100% polyester or a cotton/poly mix. The advantage of using a polyester thread is that it is very durable and won't be permanently discoloured if the indigo colour bleeds. A possible disadvantage is the slightly plastic sheen of a polyester thread, whereas a thread with cotton tends to look more rustic.

The thread size is measured in weight, with heavy thread for domestic sewing machines usually being in the Tex 60 to 80 range, with Tex being a standard measuring method for thread weight. The higher the Tex number, the heavier the thread is. On factory-made jeans, the thread is often thicker than that, but it can be hard for regular sewing machines to sew with such heavy thread.

REGULAR SEWING MACHINE THREAD

Instead of heavy thread, a similar effect can be achieved by using two spools (or bobbins) with regular sewing machine thread. The thickness is very similar to the look of a stitch sewn with heavy thread, and it's a great option when you can't locate heavy thread in the colour that you want. It can also be easier to stitch compared with heavy thread.

BOBBIN THREAD

For best results on a domestic sewing machine, use regular all-purpose sewing machine thread in the bobbin because it's hard to get the heavy thread to run smoothly through a regular bobbin, and it can also cause tension issues. An option if you do want to use heavy thread in the bobbin is to buy a spare bobbin and experiment with the tension spring, which is usually regulated with a screw.

Some machine brands also have a special bobbin for thicker thread, which might be worth trying.

PRESSER FEET FOR TOPSTITCHING

A standard presser foot will usually suffice for topstitching, but there are two additional feet that might be worth investing in. If you are having problems sewing an even line when topstitching close to an edge or a seam, check and see if your sewing machine brand has an edge stitch or edge guide foot. The foot has a blade or an extension piece that you align with the edge, which makes sewing parallel seams a breeze because you won't have to gauge with your eye or control the fabric as much as you would with a regular presser foot.

Another option to explore is a topstitching foot. It has a narrow needle opening and is constructed to sew smoothly over thick layers of fabric. On some machine brands, such as Bernina, it's best combined with a straight stitch plate

STITCH LENGTH

Use a longer stitch length when topstitching jeans. It will look more professional, and it's also easier to achieve a nice even stitch when the length is longer. There is no magic number for the perfect stitch length, but aim for around 4 mm as a starting point.

Just as a short stitch length on denim will look odd, a stitch that is too long can also look a bit off because it might not form properly and look more like a basting stitch. The thickness of the seam and the fabric properties will also influence how the stitches form, so test different settings and see what works best.

LEVEL THE PRESSER FOOT

A presser foot needs to be horizontal to properly form stitches. But when topstitching denim there will be several elevated areas, such as the back pockets, belt loops and bulky seams.

To solve this issue, you need to level the presser foot so that it doesn't point down or upwards. Use a tool like a hump-jumper (jean-a-ma-jig) to raise the slanted side of the presser foot so that it becomes horizontal again.

In many instances, simply folding a piece of the fabric underneath the presser foot will be enough to level it. Experiment and see which method you prefer.

Some presser feet also have a built-in level function that can be adjusted with a knob.

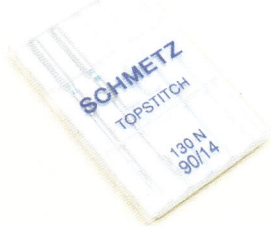

NEEDLES

Use either a larger denim needle or a special topstitching needle with a bigger eye to better accommodate thick threads. Both needle types are made for sewing through thick layers of fabric.

TENSION

Heavier thread often requires adjusting the needle tension to form a balanced stitch, which is also true for machines with auto-tension capabilities.

Always do test samples on the fabric you plan to use, and make sure you sew over the corresponding number of layers to fully gauge the right settings. The number of layers will also affect the tension settings.

Needle tension is too loose. The needle thread forms loops on the wrong side.

Needle tension is too tight. Visible bobbin thread knots on the right side.

Tension is balanced. The needle and bobbin thread are tied together evenly.

HOW TO TOPSTITCH

- Start with the needle down and pull the threads to the back. This will prevent the thread from getting tangled up, which is a common occurrence when sewing with heavy thread.

- Sew slowly and guide the fabric gently with your hands. High-speed sewing can lead to uneven stitching, especially over bumpy areas.

- If you need to stop and adjust or insert a hump-jumper, always stop with the needle down in the fabric because this will keep the stitching even and straight.

- If you are having problems with draglines and puckering, which can happen especially with lighter and stretchy denim, stitch both rows in the same direction. That said, a little ripple effect on topstitched jeans is not necessarily a bad thing because it's often part of the classic denim look.

- To secure the thread, instead of backstitching, which creates a bulky seam, just shorten the stitch length substantially when ending the stitch. To add even more security, finish the stitch with bar tacks (see page 64).

SEWING FLAT-FELLED SEAMS

Flat-felled seams are made by stitching pieces together with different seam allowances. The shorter seam allowance is encased in the wider allowance to create a durable and flat seam that is very popular for jeans. Common uses for a flat-felled seam on jeans are the inseam, the yoke and the back crotch.

To see examples of this, just look inside any ready-to-wear jeans, and you'll most likely find flat-felled seams.

In the garment industry a flat-felled seam is sewn using a special folding device, but you can mimic the look using home sewing equipment if you follow the methods described in this section.

SEAM ALLOWANCES FOR FLAT-FELLED SEAMS

If you want to do flat-felled seams the proper way, you need to adapt the pattern by using different seam allowances.

The piece on top (which is topstitched) should have around half the seam allowances as the opposite pattern piece; so, for instance, the right crotch seam allowance needs to be around twice as wide as the left crotch seam, which is placed on top on most jeans.

The seam allowances listed to the right can be adapted according to your preferences, for instance, if you want to press the yoke up rather than down.

You can also increase the width of the seam allowances to create a more substantial flat-felled seam.

GUIDE TO FLAT-FELLED SEAM ALLOWANCES

A. Right back crotch seam 24 mm (1")
B. Left back crotch seam 12 mm (½")
C. Back piece inseams 24 mm (1")
D. Upper back piece edge 12 mm (½")
E. Front piece inseams 12 mm (½")
F. Right yoke mid-back 24 mm (1")
G. Left yoke mid-back 12 mm (1")
H. Lower edge of yoke 24 mm (1")

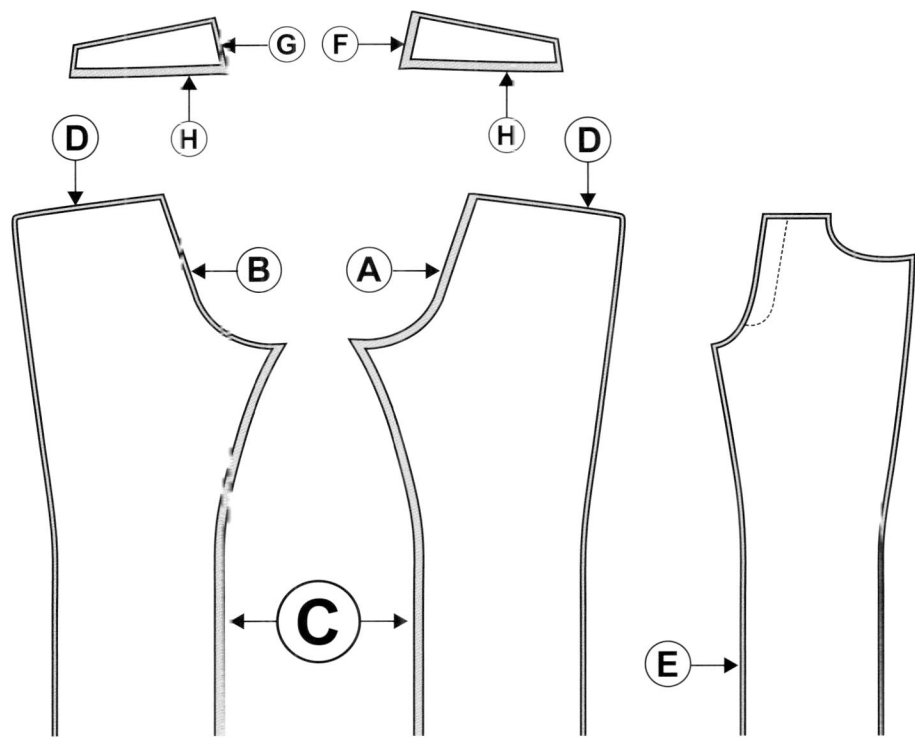

PROPER FLAT-FELLED SEAM

This method is based on the industrial way of sewing flat-felled seams on denim, using two different seam allowances, where the shorter seam allowance is enclosed in the longer one.

In a garment factory, a flat-felled seam is achieved using a special folder attachment, but a similar seam can be done on a regular sewing machine using a combination of stitching lines and pressing.

> **SUPPLIES**
> - Denim sewing machine needle (for the stitch markings)
> - Topstitching machine needle (for the topstitching)
> - Sewing machine thread for the stitch lines and bobbin thread
> - Heavy jeans thread in the needle for the topstitching

1 **Sew a marking stitch.** On all pieces with a 12 mm (½") seam allowance (A), sew a stitch marking line 10 mm from the edge (just a smidgen shorter than ½"). Use regular sewing machine thread.

2 **Fold the edge.** Press the edge towards the reverse side along the stitch line.

3 Insert the piece (B) with the longer (24 mm/1") seam allowance in the fold. Make sure the edge is all the way in and touches the fold.

4 Secure the pieces (optional). To prevent the encased piece from slipping out, open the fold and stitch together piece A and piece B. The right side of piece B should face the wrong side of A. Align with the stitched edge and sew close to the edge of piece B.

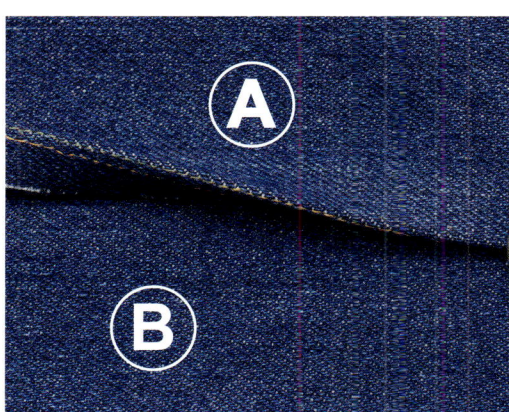

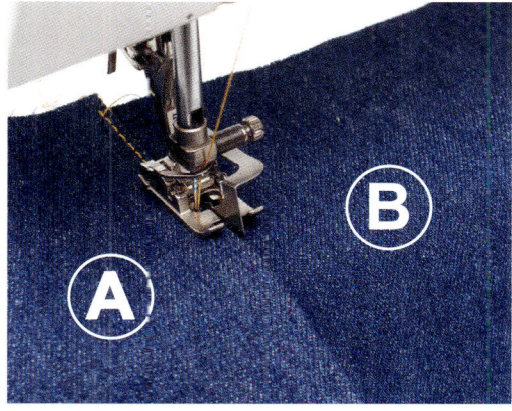

5 Fold and press to create an encased seam. Fold piece B so that it encloses the entire seam allowance of piece A. Press over the folded flat-felled area.

6 Topstitch the outer edge. Sew the first line of topstitching slightly less than 3 mm (⅛") from the edge. Pinch the seam with your fingers to make sure the seams stay folded.

7 **Topstitch the second row.** The second row of topstitching should be done around 6–8 mm from the first row and needs to hit all the layers of the flat-felled seam, so make sure you measure carefully before stitching.

8 **The finished flat-felled seam.** This method creates a beautiful flat-felled seam that can rival a professionally made seam.

9 **The reverse side.** The beauty with this method is that the reverse side will look just as neat as the right side, and the stitch lines are no longer visible because they are enclosed in the fold.

FLAT-FELLED SEAM WITH A PRESSER FOOT

Many sewing machine brands have a flat-felled presser foot that can be used to re-create a flat-felled seam on domestic sewing machines. Make sure you get the wider version of this foot, usually around 8–9 mm, so that it works with denim seams.

There is, however, one drawback with this method; on the side facing up, the first row of stitching will be bobbin thread and the second needle thread. That makes it hard to use heavy topstitching thread because the tension will most likely be unbalanced. Instead, use good quality sewing machine thread in both the bobbin and needle and make sure the tension is balanced.

The presser foot method might not work on very thick denim, so always do samples before you start flat-felling your garment.

SUPPLIES

- A wide flat-fell presser foot (usually around 8-9 mm)
- Sewing machine thread
- Denim or topstitching needle

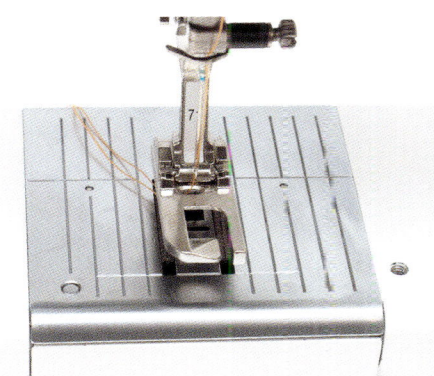

1 Set up the machine. Use regular sewing machine thread in both the bobbin and needle because both threads will be visible on the right side. Attach the flat-felled presser foot and check the presser foot instructions for recommended stitch settings.

2 Position the pieces, wrong sides facing. The bottom piece should protrude around 10–12 mm (⅜–½"), depending on the size of the presser foot. Check the instructions from the manufacturer for the specifics.

3 **Prepare for sewing.** Fold the fabric edge. Wrap the bottom edge around the upper piece to enclose the top edge. Place the folded piece underneath the presser foot. Align the outer edge with the right presser foot toe.

4 **Sew the first row.** Sew 2–3 stitches, needle down, then stop and lift the presser foot. Place the folded fabric edge in the folding extension.

5 **Stitch along the edge.** Make sure both edges are aligned with the slots of the presser foot.

6 **Press the finished seam flat.** Press so that the stitched edge is facing the fabric and is no longer visible.

7 **Prepare to sew the second row.** With the folded edge pointing to the left, insert the edge into the flat-felled extension and start sewing over the fold.

8 **Sew the second row.** Make sure both sides align, using the presser foot as your guide.

9 **The finished seam.** The lower row uses bobbin thread, and the upper shows the needle thread. This can make it a challenge to stitch a completely balanced tension seam on many machines. The advantage, however, is that this method makes it easy to sew an even seam with minimal measuring and tinkering.

STITCHING BAR TACKS

A bar tack is a dense stitch that reinforces areas that need to be very durable, such as zippers, pockets, button flies, belt loops and crotch areas. In the garment industry, this stitch is sewn using a special machine, but you can achieve a similar stitch on your home sewing equipment.

MACHINE SETTINGS

Set your machine to a tight zigzag stitch with a shorter stitch width and length.

Length: 0.3–0.5 mm

Width: 2–2.5 mm

You can also do bar tacks with a straight stitch; sew two to three parallel rows by pivoting and stitching the same distance back and forth several times.

These settings are only suggestions; always test the stitch settings on samples using several layers of your planned fabric to verify that the seam will work. If the machine is getting stuck and not feeding correctly, which can happen when sewing tacks with heavy thread on thick denim, increase the stitch length slightly.

LEVEL THE PRESSER FOOT

When sewing bar tacks over uneven areas, such as back pockets and belt loops, you need to keep the presser foot horizontal; otherwise the machine can't feed properly, and skipped stitches may occur. Folding a piece of the fabric underneath the presser foot can be enough to level it.

THREAD OPTIONS

Thread the needles with heavy thread or two strands of regular sewing machine thread. In the bobbin it's safest to use regular all-purpose thread because this will prevent the stitching from getting tangled.

You can also use a tool called hump-jumper (or jean-a-ma-jig) to raise the slanted side of the presser foot.

As for thread colour, you don't have to sew the tacks with traditional golden jeans thread; for instance some denim brands use unbleached white, red or blue thread to stitch the bar tacks on their jeans.

CHAPTER 5
ASSEMBLY

ORDER OF ASSEMBLY

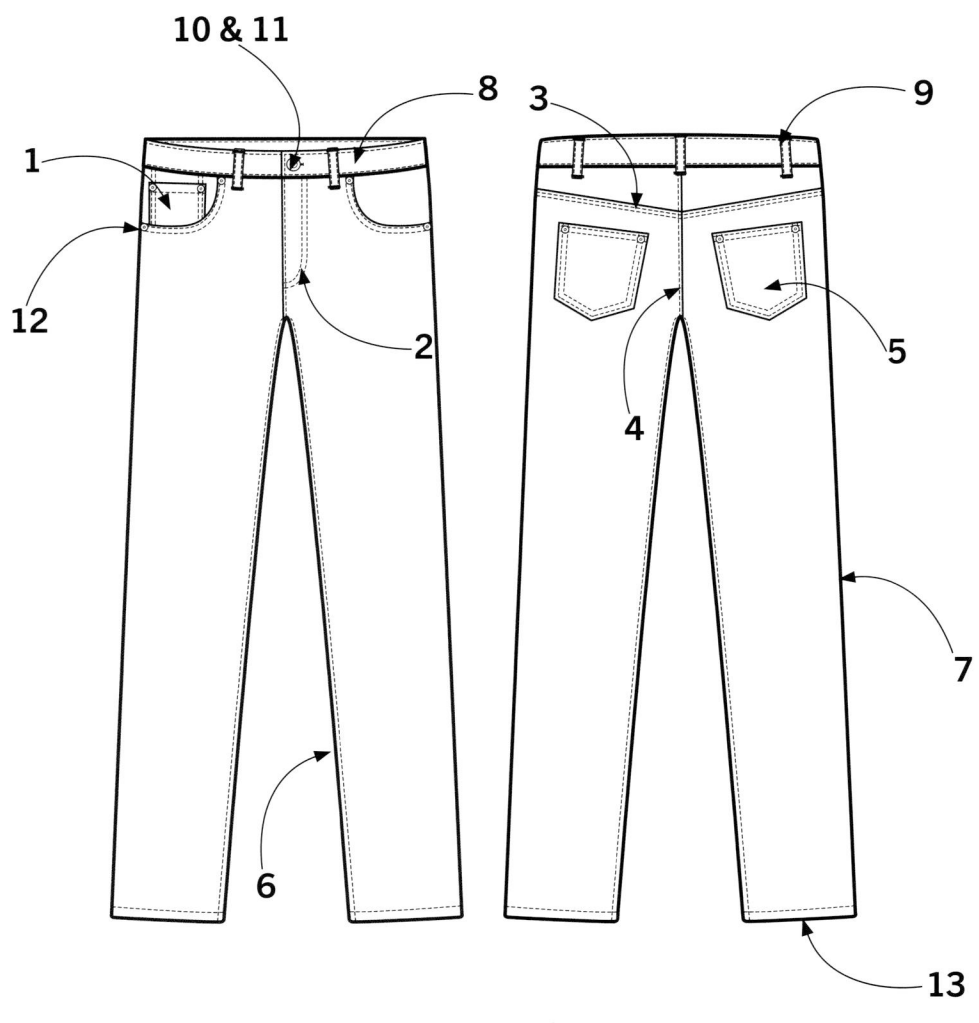

1. FRONT POCKETS
2. FLY
3. YOKE
4. BACK CROTCH SEAM
5. BACK POCKETS
6. LEG INSEAM
7. OUTSEAM
8. WAISTBAND
9. BELT LOOPS
10. BUTTONHOLE
11. BUTTONS
12. RIVETS
13. HEM

PRESSING DENIM

As with any sewing project, you should press the jeans' seams as you sew to ensure that the finished result is pristine. Because seams on jeans seams tend to be thick, especially on areas where they are joined, pressing the seams flat is also important to reduce bulk.

TIPS FOR PRESSING DENIM

- Press seams from the reverse side.
- Use a cotton setting for 100% denim fabrics.
- For denim mixed with Elastane and polyester, reduce the heat because those materials are more sensitive.
- Iron on a fabric scrap to test the settings.
- Use steam or a damp press cloth and press seam allowance apart. To set the press, iron a second time without steam or press cloth.
- To remove visible press marks on the right side, lift the seam allowance and press on the reverse side of the fabric to smooth out the surface.
- Shiny marks are caused by an iron that is too hot for the fibre to handle. To prevent this, lower the heat, press on the reverse side and use a press cloth to shield the fabric. Be especially careful when pressing over uneven surfaces such as pockets, belt loops, the waistband, and other areas where seams are joined.

THE CHARACTERISTICS OF AN AUTHENTIC PAIR OF JEANS

What truly makes a great pair of jeans is a hot topic among jeans connoisseurs. Within the jeans community, there's a very strong focus on details, and it's fascinating to dive into that world and learn how a seemingly small detail can make a big difference in how the jeans are perceived.

Jeans aficionados are especially keen on details that carry a strong heritage, often harking back as far as the late 19th century up to the 1950s. Workmanship and high-quality materials are also factors that play into the overall perception.

These days, many Japanese brands are held in high regard when it comes to creating quality denim with intricate detailing and a strong nod to the American heritage.

The guide on the opposite page is based on the views of a jeans professional and connoisseur who was consulted for this book. But of course, as with many things in life, opinions on this topic will vary!

BUTTONS

Type: Metal donut (open in the middle) or flat top button.

Metal: Brass, copper or matte silver coating.

Buttonholes: Keyhole sewn with heavy buttonhole thread.

BELT LOOPS

Technique: Two-needle coverstitch or folded and top stitched with a single row straight stitch.

Bar tack: A narrow zigzag with a short stitch length.

WAISTBAND

Stitch: Straight stitch or a combination of chainstitch and straight stitch.

Shape: Rectangular.

BACK POCKETS

Topstitching: Two rows of straight stitches

Bar tack: A narrow zigzag with a short stitch length.

Rivets: Hidden or no rivets.

Pocket decoration (arcuate): Curves, arcs, waves or other decoration, using straight stitching or done with hand painting.

FRONT POCKETS

Stitch: Two rows of chainstitch.

Coin pocket: Pocket opening made with folded selvedge denim.

Rivets: Brass metal at the corner of each seam.

POCKET LINING

Seams: French seams.

Lining: 100% unbleached cotton twill.

SIDE SEAMS

Outer leg seam: Pressed open selvedge or an overlocked seam. Seam allowance around 12 mm (½") wide.

Inner leg seam: Flat felled, sewn from the bottom of the left leg to the right leg opening.

Bar tack: A narrow zigzag with a short stitch length or a straight stitch to secure front pocket on the outer seam.

FABRIC

Weave: 3X1 twill weave (3 navy warp threads for every white weft thread)

Dye: Indigo dyed dark denim

Weight: 12–16 oz.

HEM

Stitch: Chainstitch

Seam allowance: 25 mm–30 mm (1 '–1¼") hem allowance, folded twice. 13–15 mm (⅝") finished width.

REGULAR FRONT JEANS POCKETS

This ready-to-wear-inspired method creates front pockets that looks like the ones big denim brands use. They are also, arguably, both easier and faster to sew than regular pants pockets.

For lining fabrics you can reuse fabrics from old shirts, especially those made of slightly heavier cotton/polyester poplin, which is similar to the fabric used to line jeans pockets in the garment industry.

If you want to sew a more advanced pocket version with a coin pocket and French seams, use the tutorial on page 76 instead.

SUPPLIES

- Durable but soft lining fabric, cotton twill or a cotton/poly blend
- Topstitching thread
- A presser foot with an edge guide (optional)
- Jeans or topstitching needles
- Pocket pattern pieces (see page 185 for how to download)

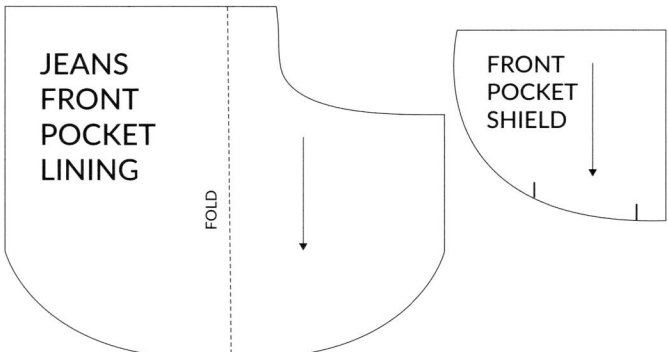

FRONT POCKET PATTERN PIECES

The front pocket pattern consists of two pieces; the pocket lining piece and the backing shield. The pocket lining piece will be folded in the middle and is attached both at the waistband and at the outer side seams. The rounded pocket shape prevents lint from getting stuck in the corners.

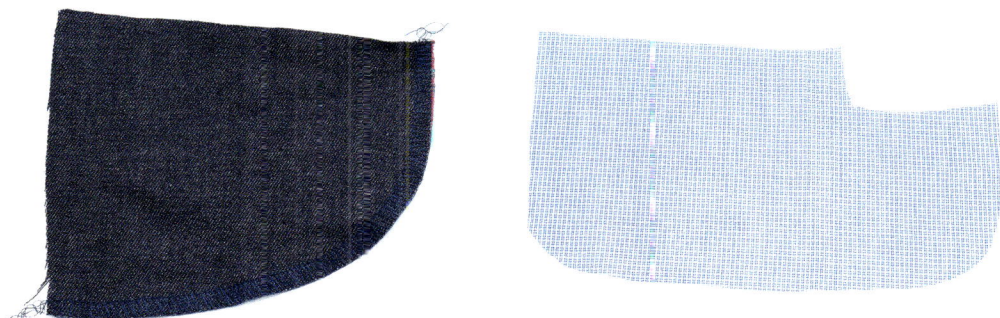

1 **Cut the pocket pattern pieces.** Serge or overcast the lower edge of the shield. **NOTE:** The edges of the lining can also be overcast at this stage, but in this tutorial it will be done at a later stage for a more time-effective assembly method.

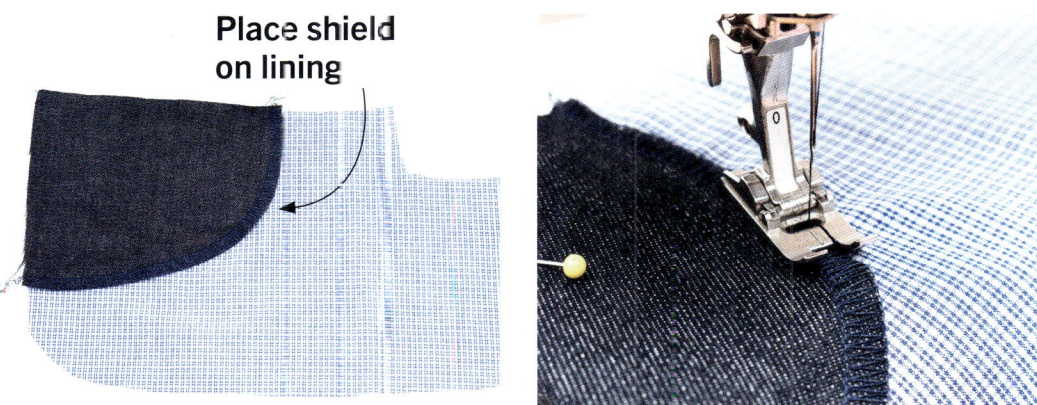

Place shield on lining

2 **Stitch the shield.** Place the backing shield on top of the lining. Attach the shield using a straight stitch over the serged edge. You can also use two rows of stitching, which is common in factory jeans making. If making a small coin pocket as well, attach that one before continuing to the next step. For instructions on how to sew a coin pocket, see pages 77–78.

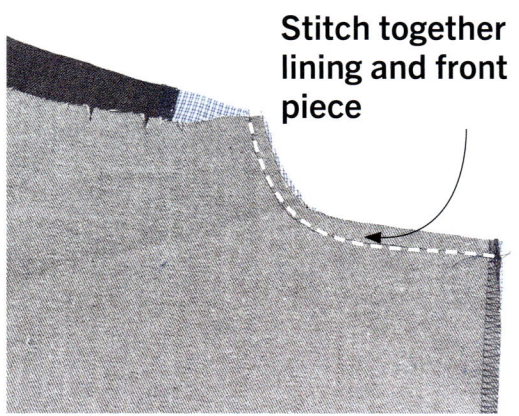
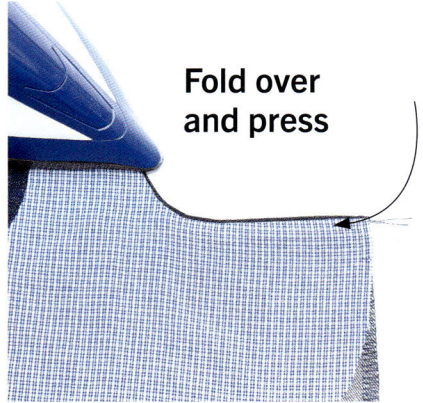

3 **Stitch the pocket lining to the front piece.** Place the lining on the pocket opening, right sides facing. Before you stitch fold the pocket to check that the shield ends up on the right side. Stitch close to the edge—a narrow seam will make shaping the opening curve easier.

4 **Fold over and press.** Let the front fabric overlap slightly to the inside so that the lining won't show through on the outside.

5 **Topstitch the pocket.** Stitch close to the edge for the first row. Using a presser foot with an edge guide can make this easier. Either stitch the second row with a regular presser foot, using the edge of the presser foot as your seam guide. Or use a regular presser foot the entire time, and sew the first and second row as a continuous seam, forming a rectangle. Just pivot when you reach the end of the first row.

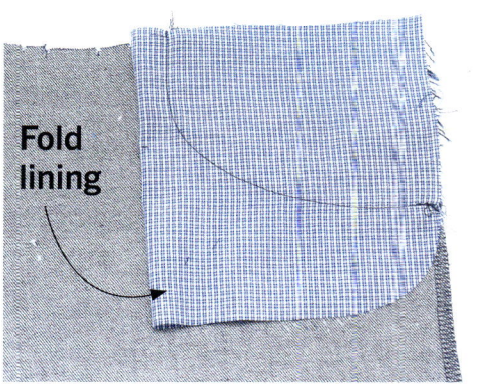 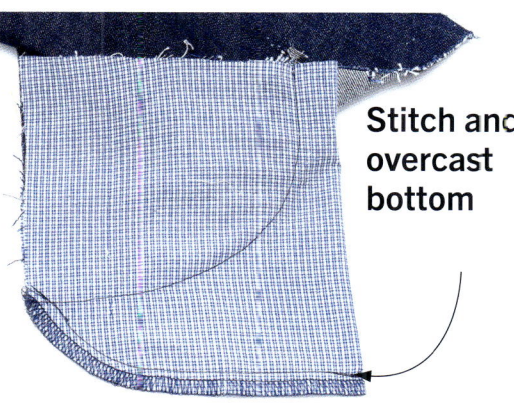

6   **Sew the bottom of the pocket.** Fold the pocket lining in the middle, and stitch along the bottom with a straight stitch. Overcast the edges after stitching the lining together.

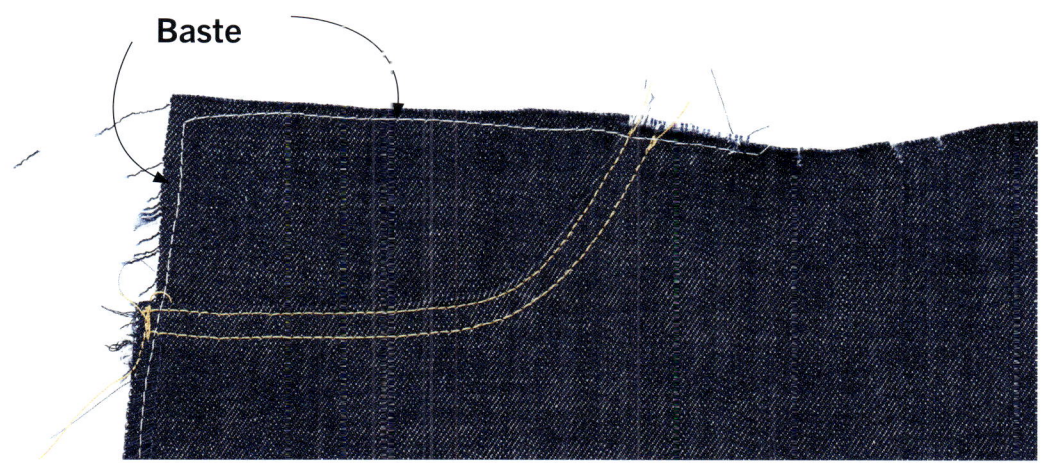

7   **Baste the pocket.** Machine-baste the side and the top in preparation for sewing the side and waist seams. Basting will keep the pocket in place during those steps in the assembly process.

CLASSIC FRONT AND COIN POCKET

For authentic-style front pockets, use this tutorial, which includes instructions for both a coin pocket and a lining sewn with French seams. This method is inspired by higher-end ready-to-wear denim and will elevate the look of your jeans.

SUPPLIES

- Lining fabric, ideally an unbleached cotton or a cotton/poly twill
- Topstitching thread
- A presser foot with an edge guide (optional)
- Jeans or topstitching needles
- Pocket pattern pieces (included in the jeans making tool kit, see page 185)

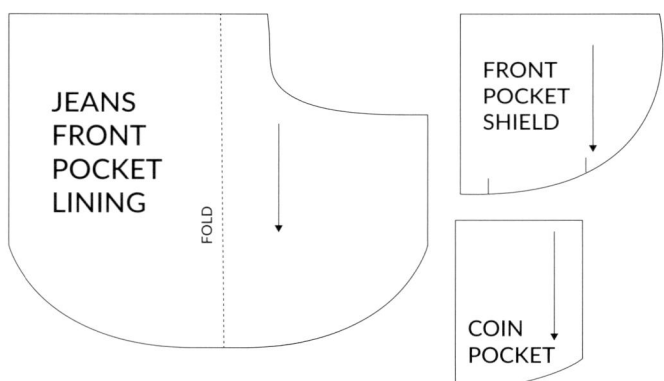

FRONT POCKET PATTERN PIECES

The front pocket pattern consists of three pieces; the pocket lining piece, the coin pocket and the pocket shield. The pocket lining piece is folded in the middle and attached to both the waistband and outer side seams. Cut two pieces of the pocket lining and the backing. Cut one coin pocket for the right backing piece.

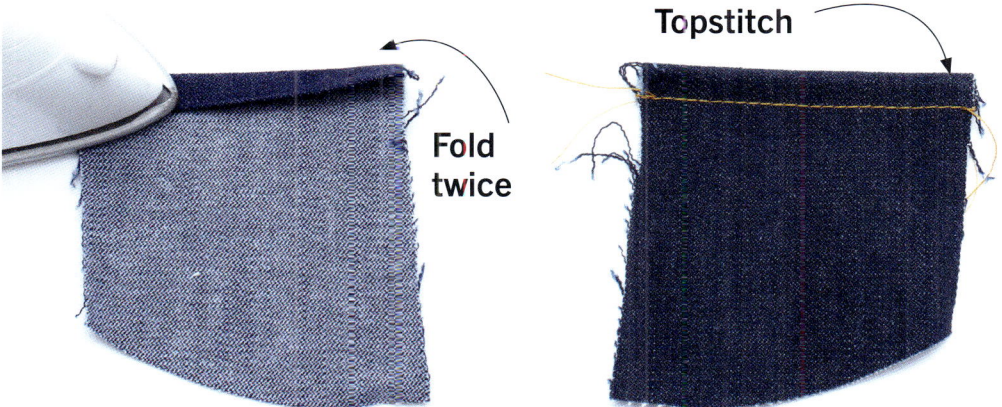

1 **Fold and topstitch the coin pocket opening.** Press the upper edge of the pocket opening with an iron, folding the seam allowance twice. Both folds should be roughly the same width. Topstitch the upper pocket edge. Use one or two rows of stitches.

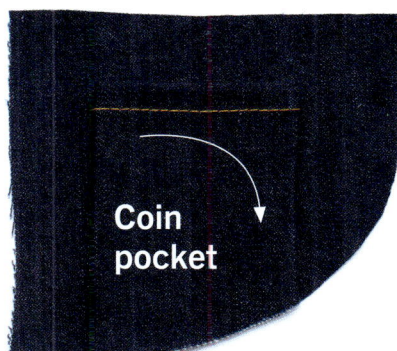

2 **Press in the side seam allowances of the coin pocket.** Make sure the seam allowances are even, and keep the iron on the same spot for a little while to set the folds. Use steam for really sharp folds.

3 **Place the coin pocket on the right-hand shield.** Align the edges with the notches if you are using the pattern pieces that are included in this book (see page 185).

FRONT POCKETS

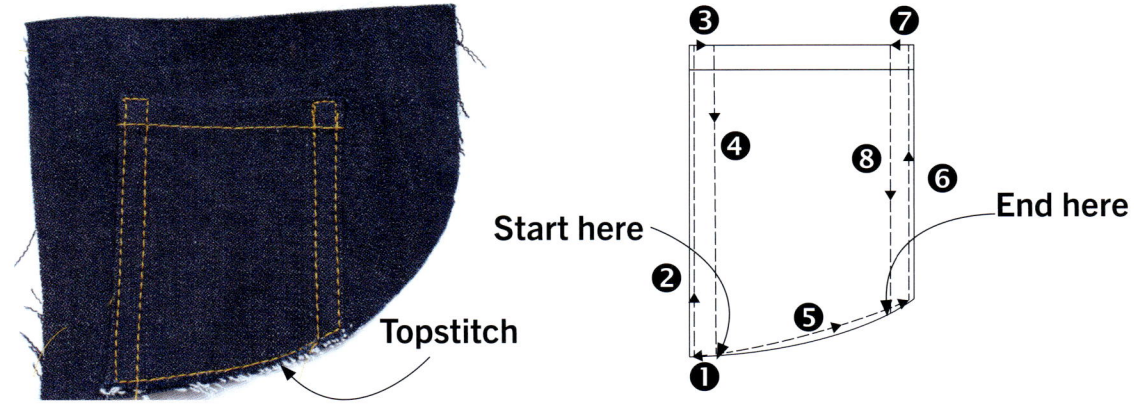

4 **Topstitch the coin pocket.** Stitch the coin pocket to the shield using topstitching thread in the needle. Sew the entire pocket as one continuous seam. Start from the lower edge (1), pivot and sew along the outer edge (2). Pivot at the top (3) and sew the inner row (4). Then turn to sew along the lower edge to close the pocket (5). Pivot at the corner and sew the outer row (6), turn again at the top (7) and finish off by stitching the inner row (8). Pivot a final time and overlap the lower edge seam using just a few stitches to secure.

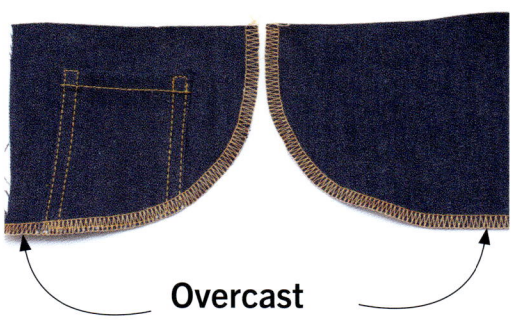

5 **Overcast the lower shield edges.** Use a 3-thread wide serger overlock stitch or a sewing machine zigzag stitch.

6 **Attach the backing shields.** Place the shield pieces on top of the lining pieces. The coin pocket should be on the right-hand pocket lining piece, and the plain backing should be on the left lining piece.

78

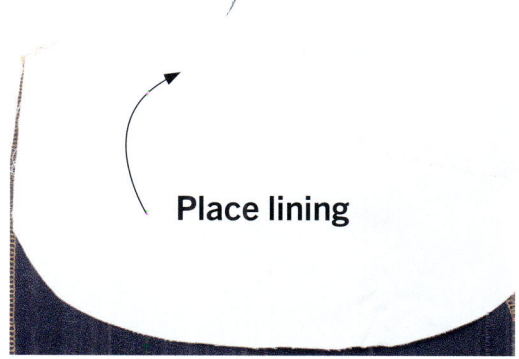

7 Attach the shield using a straight stitch over the serged edge. Sew close to edge.

8 Place the lining on the pocket opening of the front piece. Right sides facing, make sure that the pocket and the shield are on the correct side when the pocket is folded.

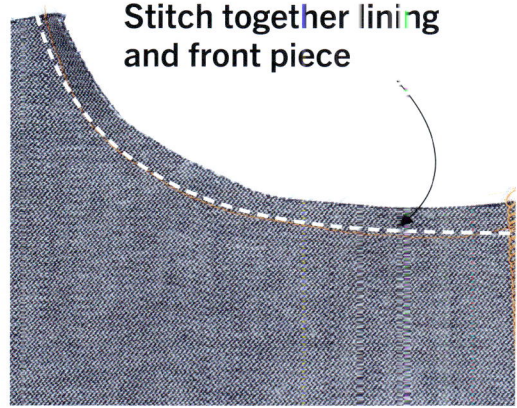

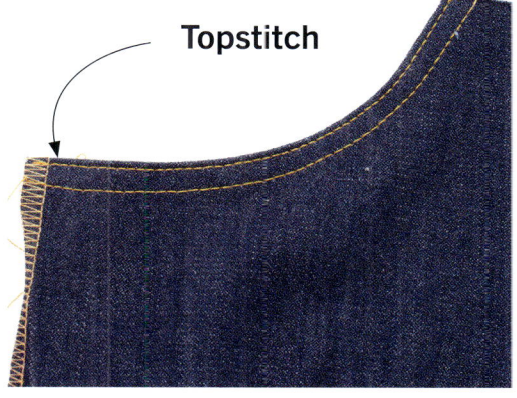

9 Stitch close to the edge. A narrow seam will make shaping the opening curve easier.

10 Fold over and topstitch. Let the front fabric overlap slightly to the inside so that the lining won't show on the outside. Topstitch the pocket. Stitch close to the edge for the first row, pivot and keep sewing the second row as a continuous seam, forming a rectangle. See *Topstitch the pocket* on page 74 for a more detailed explanation of this process.

FRONT POCKETS

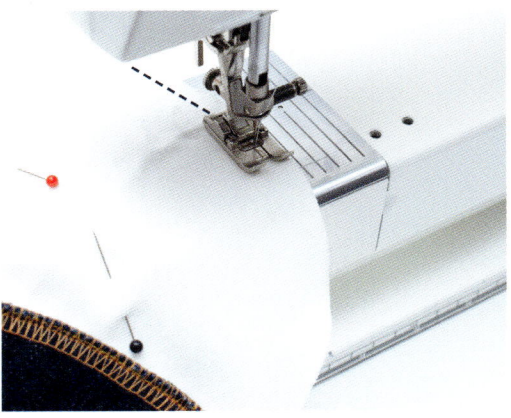

11 **Prepare for sewing a French seam at the bottom of the lining.** Fold the pocket lining in the middle, wrong sides facing. The first row of stitches should be done on the side with pocket shield facing up.

12 **Sew the first row of stitches.** Stitch a straight seam no more than 6 mm (¼") in from the edge, right side facing up.

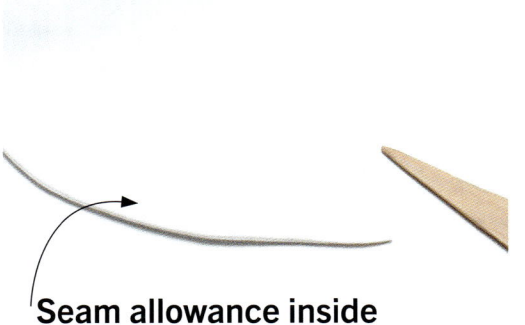

Seam allowance inside

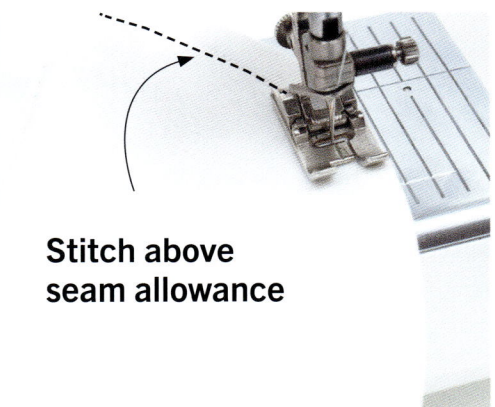

Stitch above seam allowance

13 **Turn the pocket lining.** Right sides should now be facing, with the wrong side up. Use a point turner (pictured) to smooth out the corner.

14 **Sew the second row to enclose the seam.** Stitch just above the fabric edge of the first fold so that the first seam allowance is encased in the second row of stitching. The second seam should ideally be less than 10 mm (⅜") wide, but make sure you stitch far enough in so that there is no fraying fabric peeking through.

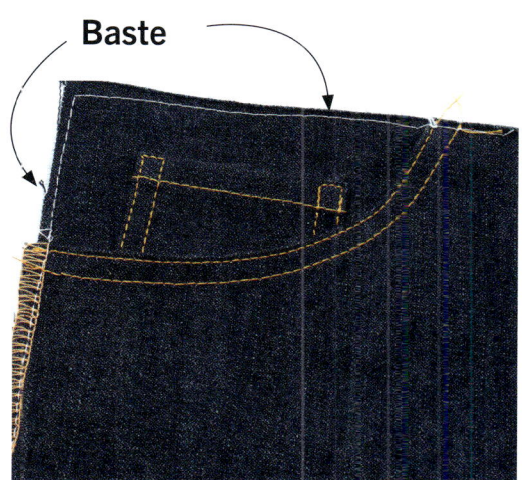

15 **Baste the pocket.** Machine-baste the side and the top in preparation for sewing the side and waist seams. Basting will keep the pocket in place during the remaining assembly process.

16 **The reverse side of the pocket.** Notice the clean look that comes with using a French seam to enclose the edge of the pocket lining.

PROFESSIONAL JEANS ZIPPER INSTALLATION

This method closely mimics the method used in the garment industry and requires a separate fly facing piece. Not all jeans sewing patterns have this piece, but you can use the downloadable facing pattern to create your own (see page 185). If your pattern has a facing extension instead of a separate piece, you can also use the *Fly facing extension* method described on page 93 to sew the jeans zipper.

SUPPLIES

- Jeans zipper
- Tracing pen (optional)
- Topstitching template (optional)
- A narrow zipper presser foot
- A presser foot with an edge guide (optional)
- Jeans or topstitching needles
- Thread and a hand sewing needle
- A pair of scissors

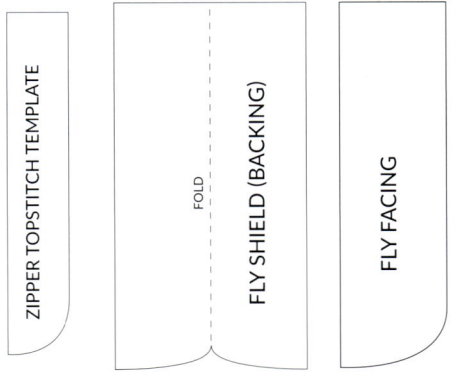

Jeans fly pattern pieces and template

The fly facing is sewn onto the left crotch after cutting (which is the traditional ready-to-wear technique for sewing the jeans fly).

A pattern for the fly shield is also needed, and a stitching template will make topstitching the zipper easier and more accurate. All pieces are included in the downloadable jeans tool kit (see page 185 for more information).

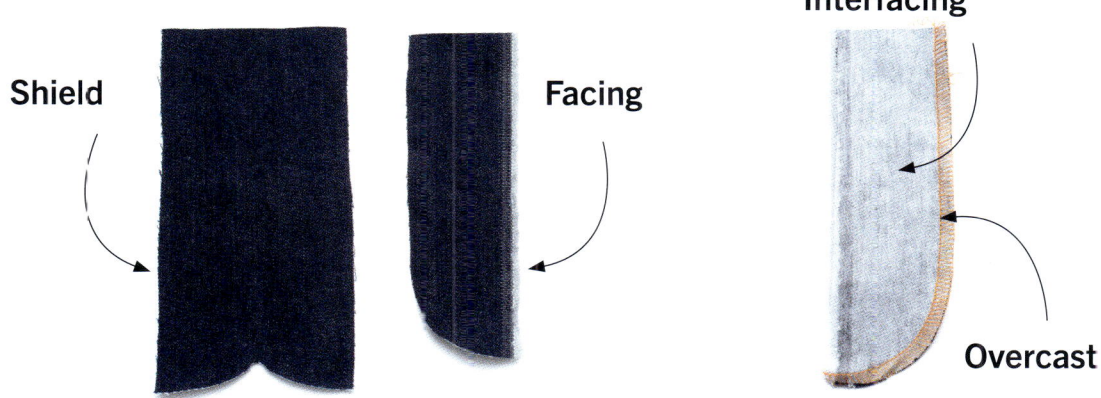

1 Cut the fly facing and shield.

2 Interface the fly facing, then overcast the round edge.

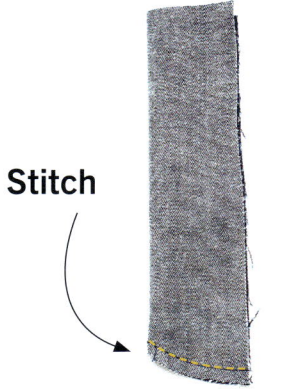

3 **Sew the fly shield.** With right sides facing, sew the bottom seam of the shield. There is no need to stitch and turn the side seam because it adds unnecessary bulk.

4 **Turn and press the shield.** Use a point turner to create a sharp corner on the shield. After pressing the shield overcast the open side.

5 **Attach the facing.** Place the fly facing along the crotch edge on the left front piece, wrong sides facing. Sew a straight stitch to attach the facing, approximately 10 mm (3⁄8") away from the edge.

6 **Press the seam.** First press the seam open. Then fold the facing under, and press over the edge to flatten the seam.

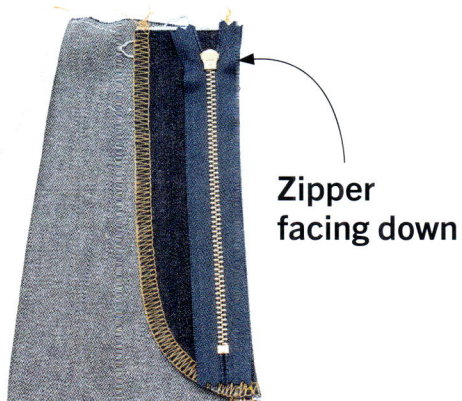

Zipper facing down

7 **Topstitch the edge.** Starting from the bottom, topstitch the facing close to the edge, around 3 mm (⅛") in.

8 **Place the zipper on the facing.** The zipper pull should face towards the fabric, and the inner zipper tape should align with the crotch edge.

9 **Stitch the zipper.** Sew a straight stitch along the edge of the outer zipper tape.

10 **Mark the outer topstitching line.** The curve should end at least 10 mm (⅜") below the zipper stop so that there's enough room for the presser foot when topstitching. Use a stitching template to make tracing easier (see page 97).

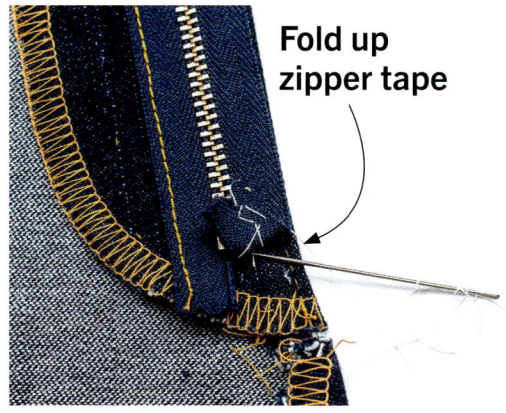

Fold up zipper tape

11 Fold away the outer zipper tape edge. Lift and fold the end of the outer zipper tape so that the topstitching doesn't catch it. Attach the fold with a few basting stitches. This is necessary for when you insert the shield later on.

12 Topstitch the fly front. Starting from the upper edge, sew the outer row first until you reach the lower edge.

13 Turn and sew the other row. When you reach the edge, with the needle in the fabric, lift the presser foot and turn the piece 90 degrees. Sew along the edge for approximately 6 mm (¼"), pivot again and sew the inner row of topstitching. The entire fly topstitching should be one continuous seam.

14 **Attach the fly shield to the zipper.** Place the outer zipper tape, with the pull facing up, along the outer edge of the fly shield.

15 **Stitch along the edge of the zipper tape.** Start from the bottom. In this step the pull side of the zipper should be facing up. Sew either one or two rows of stitcing.

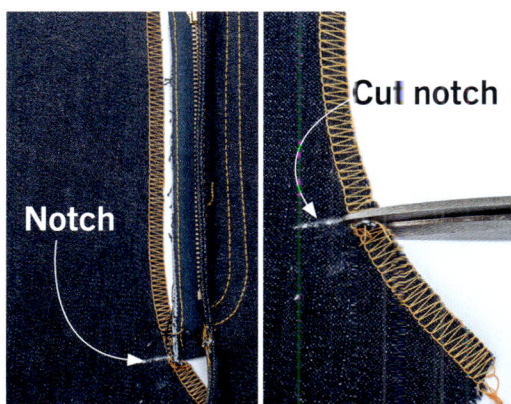

16 **Notch and cut the right-hand front piece.** Place the left facing piece parallel to the right piece. Mark a notch on the right piece where the fly facing begins on the left piece. Then cut the notch. Make the cut small, slightly less than the seam allowance.

17 **Fold in the upper seam allowance on the right piece and press.** Leave the lower seam allowance open.

FLY CLOSURES

18 **Attach the zipper.** Place the folded edge on the zipper, with a few millimetres between the fabric edge and the coils.

19 **Topstitch along the edge of the shield to secure the zipper.** Basting will make this step easier. If the zipper tape is fairly narrow, use a zipper presser foot so that the stitching doesn't catch the coils. On a wider zipper tape, a standard presser foot can be used instead.

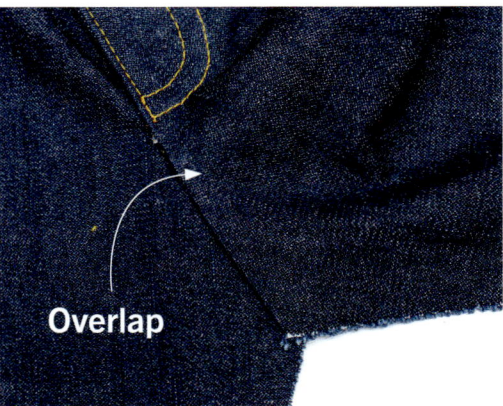

20 **Fold and press the lower edge of the left crotch.** This is in preparation for stitching together the front crotch.

21 **Place the folded edge on top of the right piece.** Align the edges of the seam allowances.

22 **Topstitch the crotch seam together.** Starting from the lower edge, stitch the first row and continue sewing so that the stitch overlaps the fly topstitching.

23 **Pivot the stitch.** With the needle in the fabric, lift the presser foot and turn the piece 90 degrees, then sew approximately 6 mm (¼").

24 **Turn again and stitch the inner row.** Use the presser foot toe as a guide to make the stitching even. The entire crotch topstitching should be one continuous seam.

25 **The finished crotch seam.** Notice how it overlaps the zipper topstitching. But you can also extend the stitching above the lower edge of the zipper stitching.

26 **The finished zipper.** Because the lower part of the zipper is secured with two rows of stitching, bar tacks are generally not necessary. But you can always add them using the methods described in the *Stitching bar tacks* section, pages 64–65.

LEFT OR RIGHT ZIPPER?

In this book, the tutorials show how to insert zipper and button flies so that they open from the right-hand side. Traditionally this how jeans are sewn, but you've probably noticed that on some pants zippers are opened from the left instead.

There is a historical reason for this variation. When button closures were introduced, they opened to the right on men's garments and to the left on clothes made for females. The context was that upper-class females had dressers, whereas men supposedly dressed themselves, which is the reason why closures on female garments were mirrored. For some reason, that tradition has stuck, even in modern times, so you can still find a lot of garments designed for females with closures that open to the left.

At the end of the day it comes down to personal preference, so if you want to sew your zipper so that it opens to the left instead, you can still follow the tutorials in this book by just exchanging left with right and vice versa.

JEANS ZIPPER WITH A FLY FACING EXTENSION

Installing a zipper on a pair of jeans requires a fair number of steps and some precise topstitching, but there is no need to feel intimidated by the process. This tutorial shows how to install a jeans zipper on a jeans pattern that has a fly facing extension and uses a mix of home sewing and ready-to-wear techniques.

SUPPLIES

- Jeans zipper
- Paper template
- Tracing pen (optional)
- A narrow zipper presser foot
- A presser foot with an edge guide (optional)
- Jeans or topstitching needles
- Thread and a hand sewing needle
- A pair of scissors

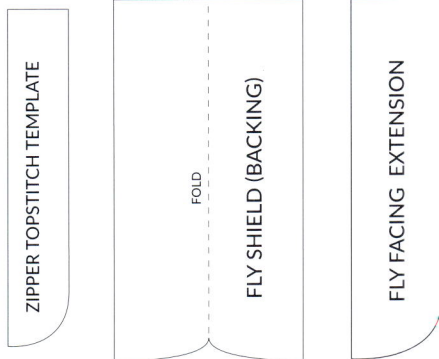

Jeans fly pattern pieces and template

The front crotch may be cut with fly facings included as one piece, or the fly facing may be sewn onto the left crotch after cutting. In this tutorial the facing is cut as an extension, removing the need for a separate facing piece.

All pieces are included in the jeans tool kit pack that you can download for free (see page 185).

FLY CLOSURES

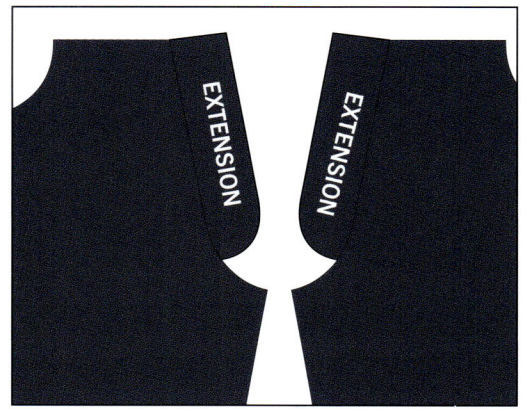

1 **Cut the front crotch with a fly facing extension on both sides.** The extension will be trimmed away on one side at a later step in the process.

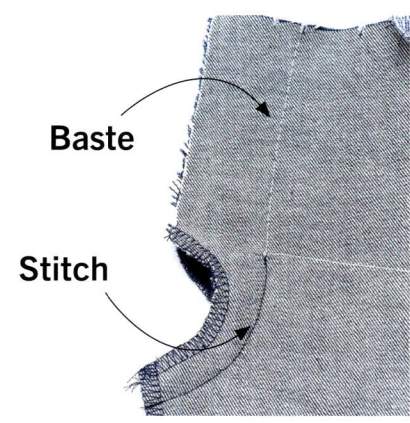

2 **Sew the front crotch.** Sew the front crotch seams together, ending where the little hole is (blue thread). Baste the remaining crotch seam (white thread).

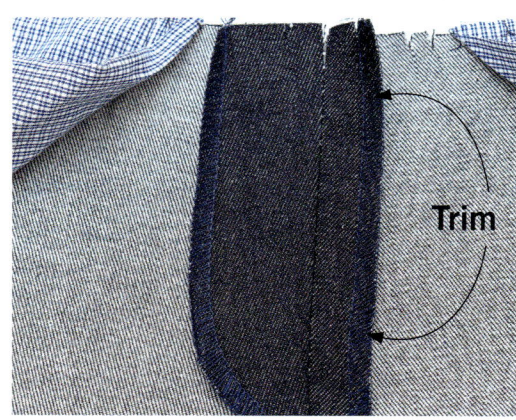

3 **Trim away the right facing if needed.** Cut away from the right-hand flap so that only a 12 mm (½") wide extension remains. Overcast the edges if you haven't done that already.

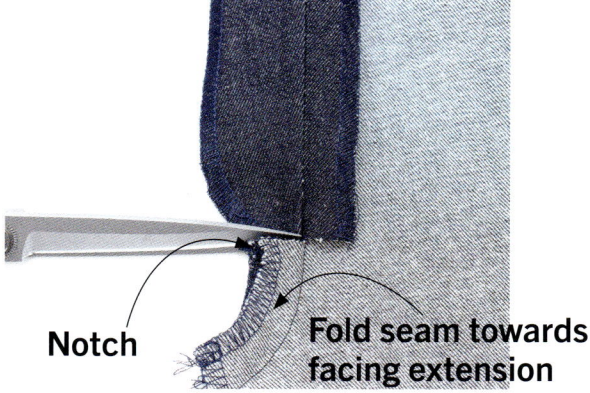

4 **Clip the crotch seam.** Clip just below the facing. The facing area should be left open and the clipped crotch seam folded towards the extension.

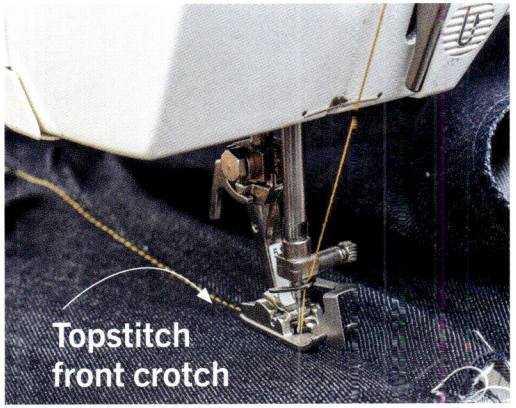
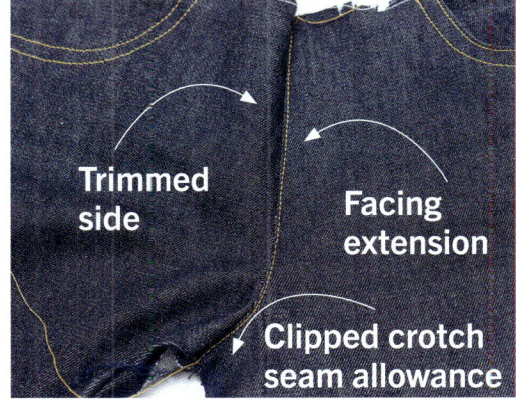

5 **Topstitch the crotch seam.** Edge stitch on the side of the facing extension. Make sure the clipped lower crotch seam is pressed towards the facing and stitched over. Using an edge presser foot makes this step easier.

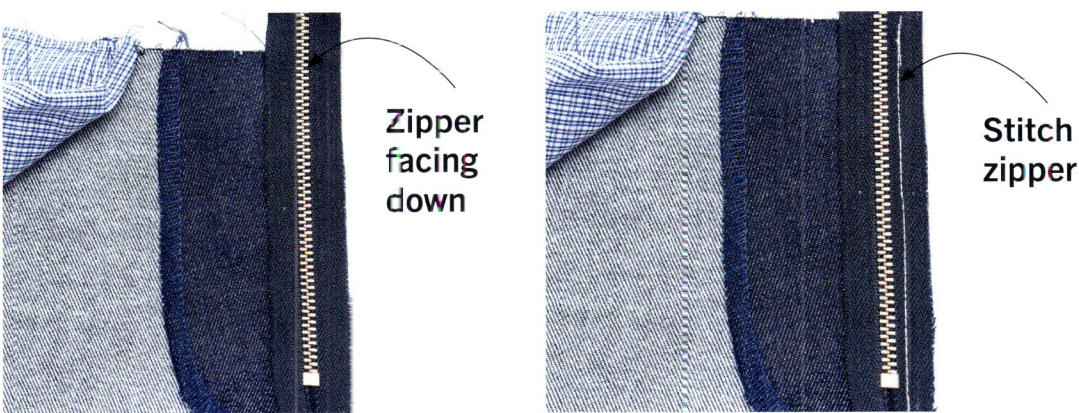

6 **Attach the zipper to the trimmed extension.** Place the zipper face down on the extension. Stitch the zipper to the extension, sewing fairly close to the teeth using a narrow zipper presser foot.

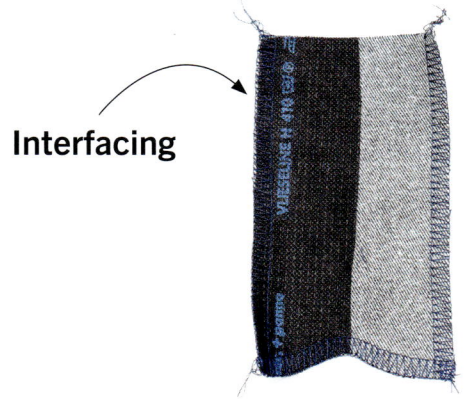

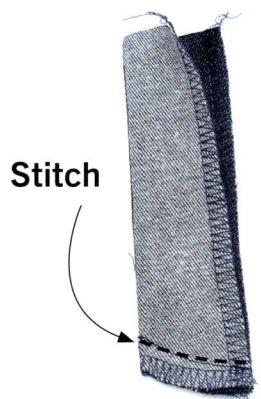

7 **Interface and overcast the fly shield.** Fuse the interfacing to one side of the fly shield. The interfacing should extend slightly over the fold. Overcast all the edges.

8 **Sew the bottom seam of the shield.** There is no need to stitch and turn the side seam because it adds unnecessary bulk. An open side on the shield is the standard method in the garment industry.

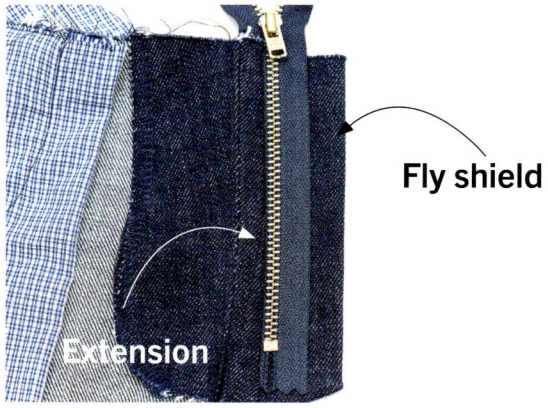

9 **Turn and press.** Use a point turner to create a sharp corner on the shield.

10 **Slide in the shield underneath the extension and zipper.** Align the inner edge of the shield with the seam allowance of the trimmed extension.

11 **Attach the shield to the zipper.** Stitch on the left side of the zipper, over the shield, zipper and trimmed extension, sewing close to edge.

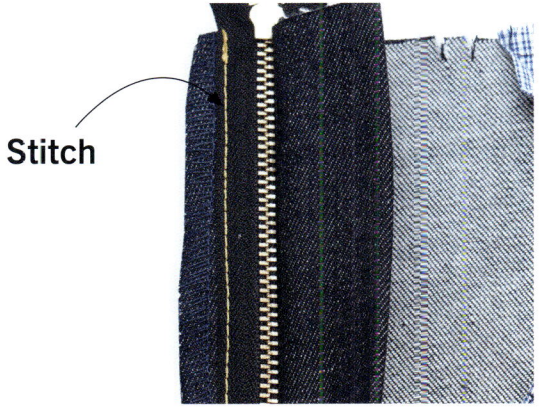

Stitch

Mark

12 **Lay the zipper towards the fly facing.** With the zipper pull facing down. Fold back the pant front body and sew the zipper tape onto the facing, but not through the jeans.

13 **Mark the outer topstitch line for the zipper.** Use a tailor's pen or tracing wheel and mark the stitch lines on the fabric using a template as a guide. You can also attach the template to the fabric with tape or Blu Tack and stitch along along the edge (see next page). That way you don't need any tracing.

FLY CLOSURES

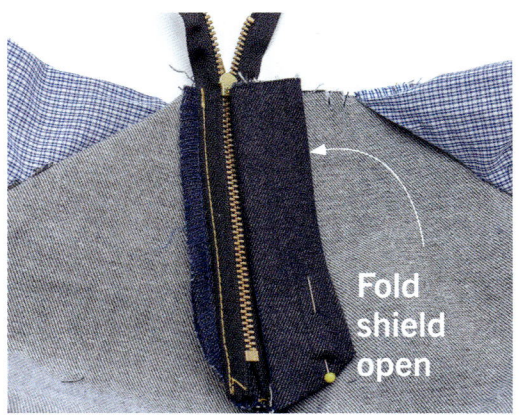

14 Fold the fly shield to the right and pin it in place. Before topstitching, the fly shield needs to be folded away so that it's not stitched over, which would prevent the zipper from being opened once sewn together.

15 Topstitch the outer zipper seam. Start from the top and stitch down along the curve. Make sure you don't stitch over the shield; it needs to be folded away during this step.

16 The first row of stitches. The end of the stitching at the crotch seam will be properly secured later with bar tacks once both rows of topstitching are done.

17 Topstitch the second row. Use the previous line of stitching as a guide. Align the first row of stitches with a spot on the presser foot, such as a corner. This will make it easier to sew the second row exactly like the first one.

18 Remove the basting.

19 Fold the fly shield back. This is in preparation for the bar tacks that will keep the lower part of the shield in place.

20 Stitch bar tacks. Starting from the crotch seam, sew narrow zigzag stitches with a short stitch width over the zipper topstitching. The bar tacks should be sewn over the shield. This step secures the crotch seam and keeps the lower edge of the fly shield in place.

For ideas on how to sew different bar tack finishes, see *Stitching bar tacks* on pages 64–65.

BUTTON FLY INSTALLATION

The button fly was the original closure on jeans and is still popular today. While it might look somewhat elaborate, installing a button fly is often easier compared to a zipper, especially if you are new to sewing jeans.

Also note that a button fly is best suited for more loose-fitting jeans because a skinny fit can cause the buttoning to pull and gape.

SUPPLIES

- Lightweight interfacing
- Tracing pen
- Jeans or topstitching needles
- Topstitching and regular sewing machine thread
- A pair of scissors
- Buttons

To sew a button fly, you'll need a fly shield and a button placket pattern piece. The topstitching template is optional but will make tracing the stitch lines of the fly easier. All pieces are included in the downloadable jeans tool kit pack (see page 185 for more information).

Jeans button fly pattern pieces and stitch template

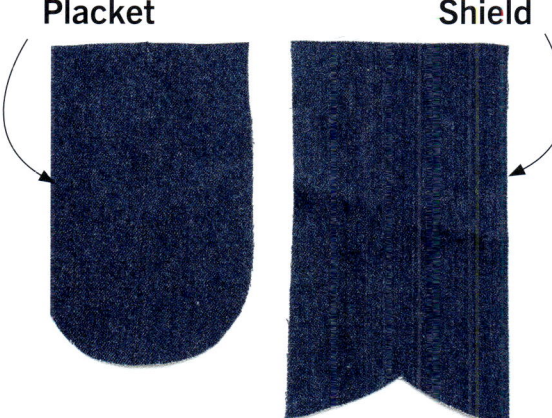

Placket   Shield

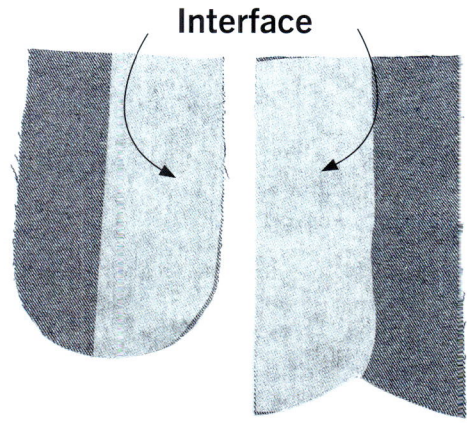

Interface

1 **Cut the button placket and fly shield.** If your pattern lacks button fly pattern pieces, use the downloadable patterns provided with this book (see page 185) and adjust the length if needed.

2 **Interface the pieces.** If the denim is light to medium weight and/or has stretch, interface the side that is facing towards the body using a lightweight fusible. Let the edge of the interfacing extend slightly over the center part for a crisp fold.

Stitch

3 **Sew the fly shield.** With right sides facing, sew the bottom seam of the shield. The long side should remain open. Turn and use a point turner to create a sharp corner on the shield.

4 **Press the shield and placket.** Right sides up, wrong sides facing.

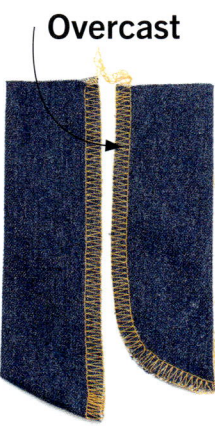

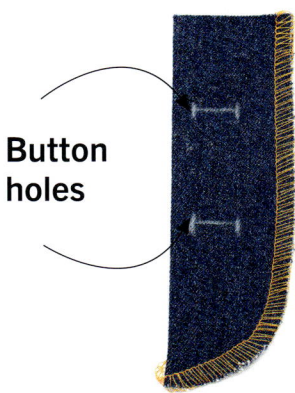

5 **Overcast the edges.** Using an overlock or zigzag stitch, overcast the open edges of the placket and shield. The upper edges can be left raw because they will be enclosed in the waistband.

6 **Mark the buttonholes.** Add two to four buttonholes on the placket. The highest button should be around 20–25 mm (¾"–1") below the upper edge seam allowance. Place the lowest button around 60 mm (2 ⅜") above the end tip of the placket. Space the buttons evenly, and let the buttonholes end approximately 6–10 mm (¼–⅜") in from the folded edge.

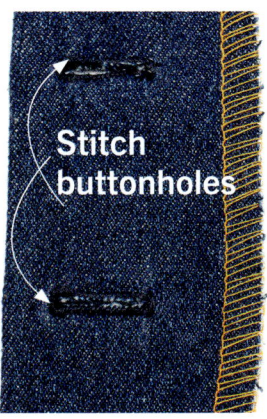

7 **Stitch the buttonholes.** See *Sewing buttonholes* on pages 163–165 for detailed instructions on how to sew buttonholes on jeans.

8 **Cut a notch below the placket.** Place the placket on the left-hand front piece, aligning it with the edges of the fabric. Cut a 6 mm (¼") long notch underneath the placket. The notch should be equal to one half of the total seam allowance.

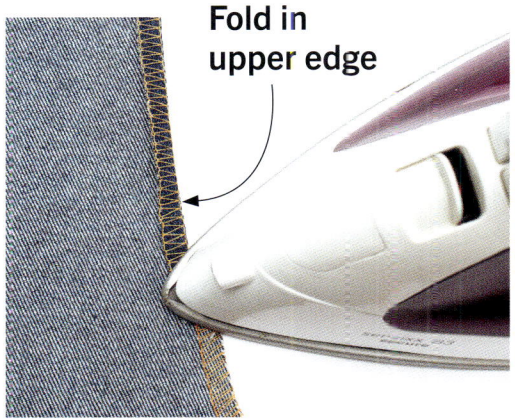

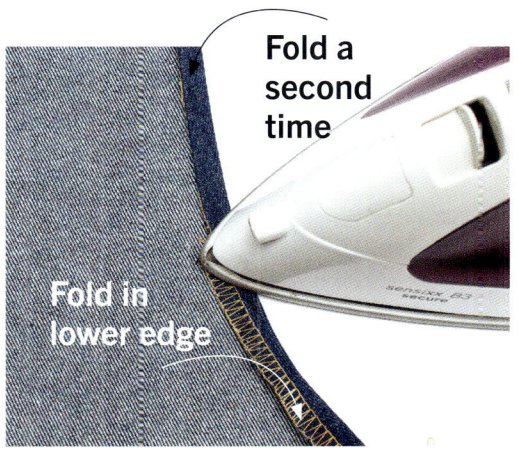

9 **Fold and press the upper edge of the crotch seam.** The fold should be as wide as the notch. Note that you are doing this on the left-hand front piece.

10 **Fold and press again.** This time the entire edge should be folded so that the upper part is folded twice and the lower part, beneath the notch, is folded once.

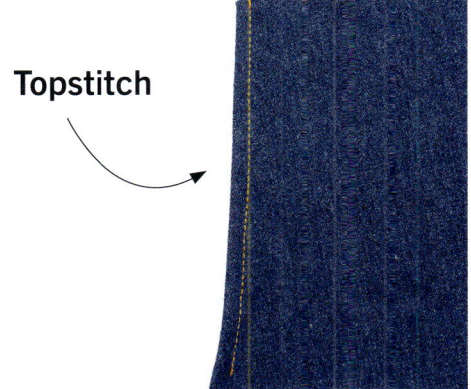

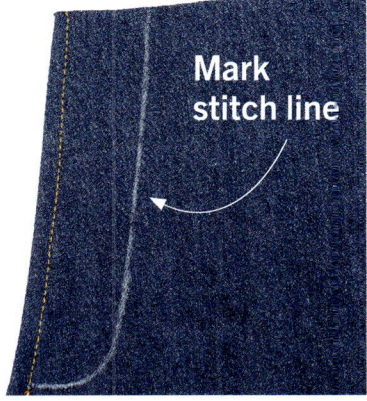

11 **Topstitch the fly edge.** Sew a stitch over the twice-folded area using topstitching thread in the needle and regular sewing machine thread in the bobbin.

12 **Mark the outer topstitching row on the left fly piece.** Before you move on to the next step, place the placket on top of the markings to make sure that the stitching will catch the outer edge of the placket (very important).

13 **Place the placket on the reverse side.** The edge of the placket should be moved inwards so that there is about a 5 mm (slightly less than ¼") difference between placket and the folded and stitched edge.

14 **Topstitch the fly.** Start by stitching the outer row, making sure the stitch catches the placket underneath.

15 **Pivot at the lower edge.** With the needle still down in the fabric, pivot 90 degrees and stitch upwards for around 5–6 mm (slightly less than ¼").

16 **Pivot again and stitch the second row.** Use the outer edge of the presser foot as a guide to make sure the rows are evenly spaced.

17 **Attach the shield.** With the shield facing the right side of the right front piece, stitch along the edge. The seam width should be slightly less than the seam allowance for this area.

18 Fold back and press the shield.

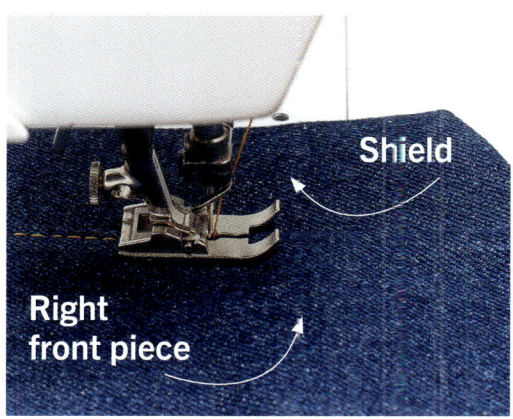

19 **Edge stitch the shield.** Using topstitching thread in the needle, stitch down the shield sewing close to the edge.

20 Fold and press in the crotch seam allowance.

21 **Align the placket with the shield.** Place the placket side (left-hand piece) on top of the shield (right-hand piece). The edge of the left piece should extend over the stitched line of the shield, but not much, ideally slightly less than 5 mm (a little less than ¼"). Pin the layers together.

22 **Place the left folded seam allowance on top of the right front piece.** The crotch seam will be joined using topstitching and won't be sewn together like a regular seam.

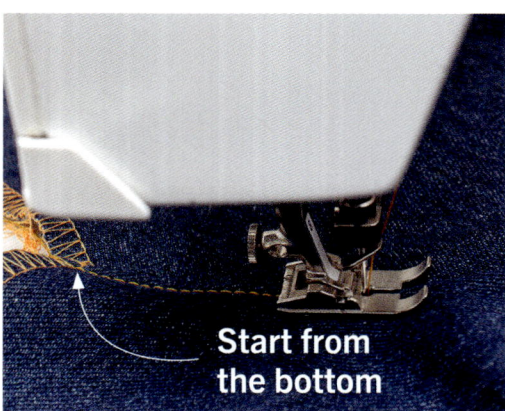

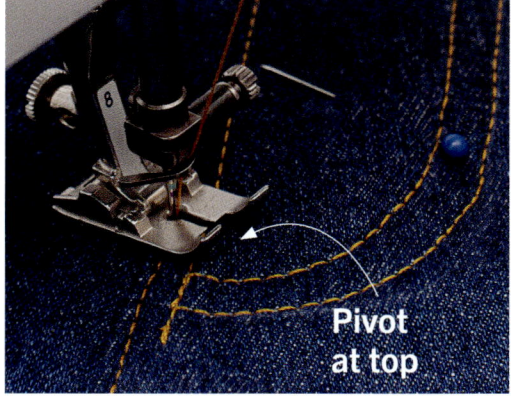

23 **Topstitch the crotch seam together.** Starting from the lower edge, stitch the first row along the edge and continue sewing so that the stitch overlaps the fly topstitching.

24 **Pivot the stitch.** Once you have passed the lower edge of the placket, pivot and sew approximately 6 mm (¼"), either horizontally or diagonally.

25 **Turn again and sew the inner row of topstitching.** Use the presser foot toe as a guide to making the stitching even. The entire crotch topstitching should be one continuous seam.

26 **Stitch a bar tack to reinforce the seam.** Use a narrow zigzag stitch with a shorter stitch length. Stitch just above the curved area where the shield and placket overlap. See *Stitching bar tacks* on pages 64–65 for detailed instructions.

27 **Attach the buttons to the shield.** For detailed instructions on how to insert denim buttons, check out the button tutorials on pages 166–169.

28 **The finished button fly.** While this process involves a fair amount of steps, the actual assembly is straightforward and not that hard to do, even if this is your first time sewing a button fly.

BACK POCKETS

With the right tools and preparation, sewing jeans back pockets is a fairly easy thing to do. The trick is to use a pressing template as your guide when shaping the pockets. This will create beautiful pockets with razor-sharp corners.

You can either sew the back pockets before the yoke and crotch seams are sewn, or afterwards if you want to experiment with placements, which is easier once the other seams are already sewn.

SUPPLIES

- Paper board for the pressing templates
- Tracing pen or another marking tool
- Topstitching thread
- Edge presser foot
- Jeans or topstitching needles

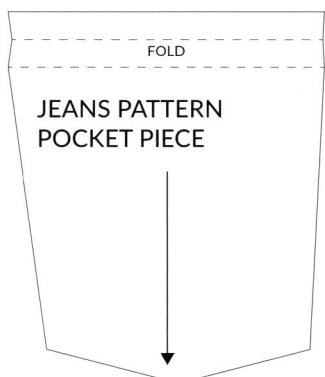

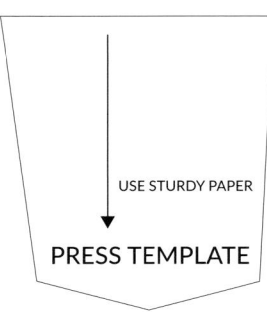

Back pocket pattern pieces

The back pocket pattern pieces jeans are included in the downloadable tool kit (see page 185) and consists of two pieces: the pocket piece and the press template, which is the same shape as the pocket but with the seam allowances removed. To cut the templates use any firm paper, such as a cereal box, the back of a legal pad or some other stable paper board.

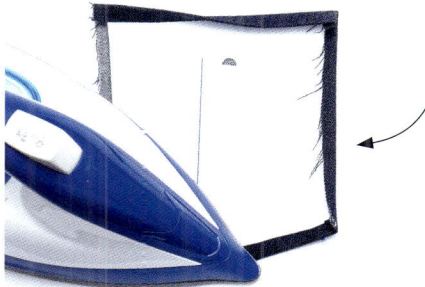

1 **Prepare the pockets and template.** Cut out the cardboard template the same size as the finished pocket. Overcasting the edges of the pocket is not necessary; the topstitching is enough to stop the fraying.

2 **Shape the pockets using the template.** Start by folding and pressing the upper edge of the pocket opening with an iron, then fold the seam allowance twice. Shape and press the remaining sides, making sure the corners are sharp.

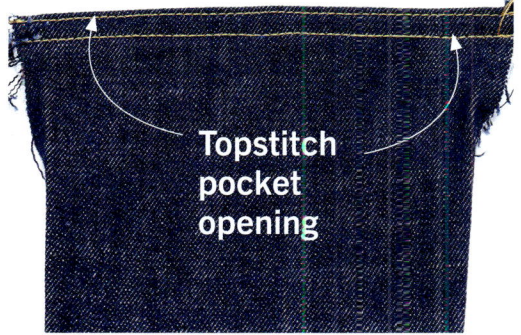
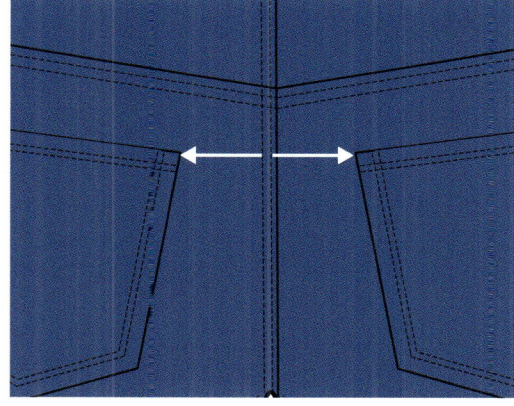

3 **Topstitch the upper pocket edge.** Sew one or two rows of stitches. You can sew both rows as a continuous seam, forming a rectangle.

4 **Place the pockets.** On jeans, the center back topstitching, and not the actual seam ditch, should be your guide. Aim to have around the same distance between the left stitching and left pocket as you have with the right topstitching and right pocket. Experiment and see what looks good to your eye. See *Back pocket placement* on pages 114–115 for more ideas.

BACK POCKETS

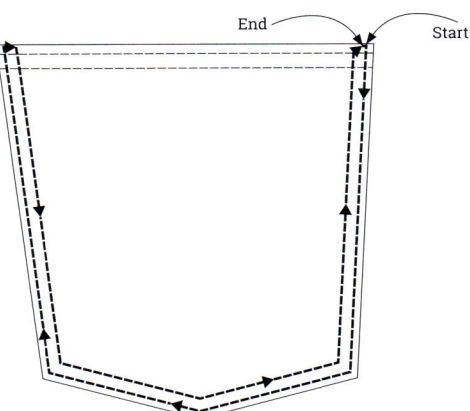

5 Pin pockets in place. Measure the distance from both the backstitching and the yoke to ensure the placement is even on both sides. Pin the pocket pieces in place, using just a few pins so that they won't get in the way when sewing.

6 Sewing order for topstitching a back pocket. For the most secure assembly, stitch both rows as one continuous seam, following the arrows in the diagram. Overlap to secure.

Outer edge

7 Topstitch the outer row. Pin the pocket in place using just one or two needles in the middle. Then topstitch the pocket into place. Start with the outer row, using the edge of the pocket as the guide. Keep sewing until you reach the upper edge of the opposite side.

8 Stitch the second row. If you are topstitching in one continuous sequence, pivot at the top edge and keep sewing the inner row. Use the outer edge of the presser foot as a guide, placing it along the first row of stitching. Finish off by overlapping the outer row, and reduce the stitch length when overlapping to secure the seam without the need for backstitching.

9 **The completed topstitching.** For even more security, either stitch bar tacks (see next step) or attach rivets (page 160) at the top corners of the pockets.

10 **Sewing bar tacks.** Stitch a narrow zigzag with a shorter stitch length either horizontally or diagonally to secure the corners of the pocket See page 64 for more detailed instructions on how to sew bar tacks. **TIP:** Fold the fabric or use a hump-jumper to level the presser foot for better feeding.

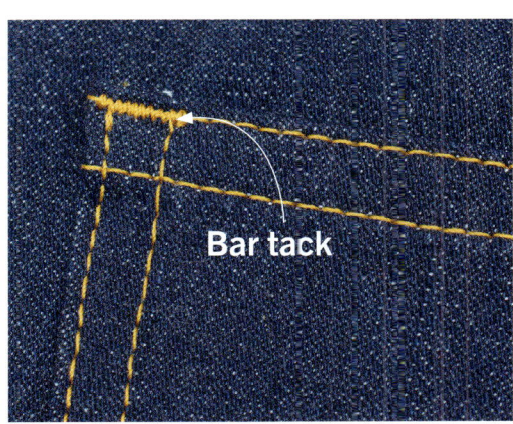

11 **The finished tack.** Don't worry if the bar tack stitches look a bit rough. Many jeans aficionados actually prefer this look, and it can also be hard to achieve good denim tack stitches on a domestic sewing machine. Also, increasing the stitch length can help a lot with the feeding on thick layers.

12 **The finished pocket.** Using this method with a press template and sewing the entire topstitching in one sequence ensures a beautifully shaped and very durable back pocket.

BACK POCKET PLACEMENTS

The placement, shape and style of the back pockets can have a substantial impact on how the backside looks visually. Here are some suggestions on how to create the specific look you are going for.

RESULT SMALLER BUTT

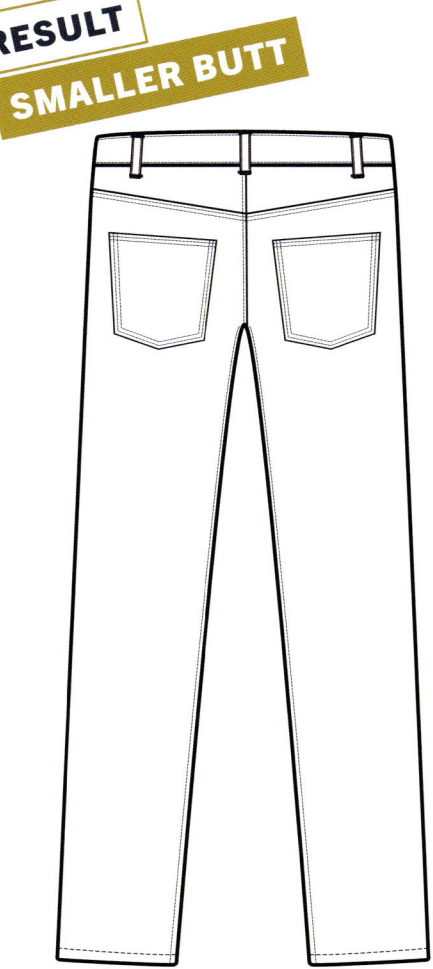

Stick to simple pockets with no flaps or heavy decoration. Opt for a larger pocket size and lower them so that they end at the thigh, rather than on the curved part of the butt.

RESULT ROUNDER BUTT

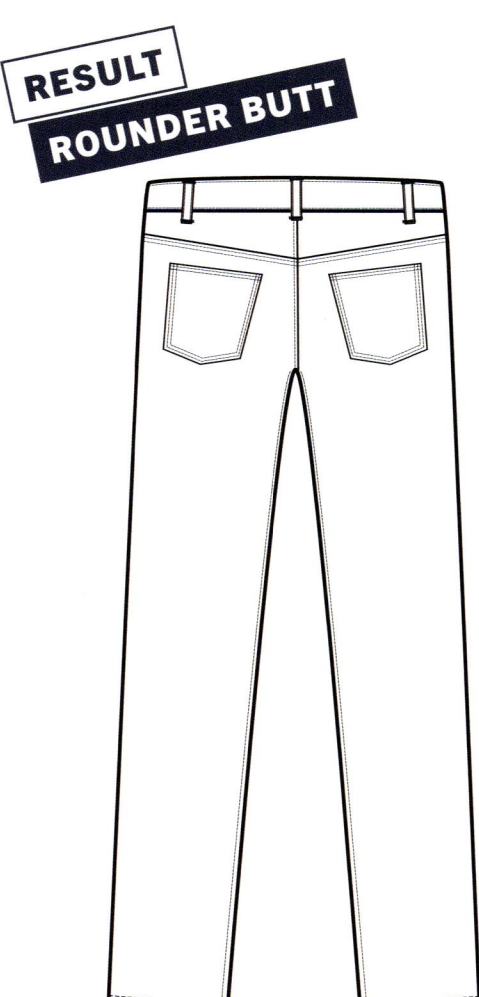

Pick a smaller pocket size. The pockets should end on your butt, above the bottom butt curve, and not below it. Use a pocket shape that is slanted on the inside.

RESULT
FLATTER BUTT

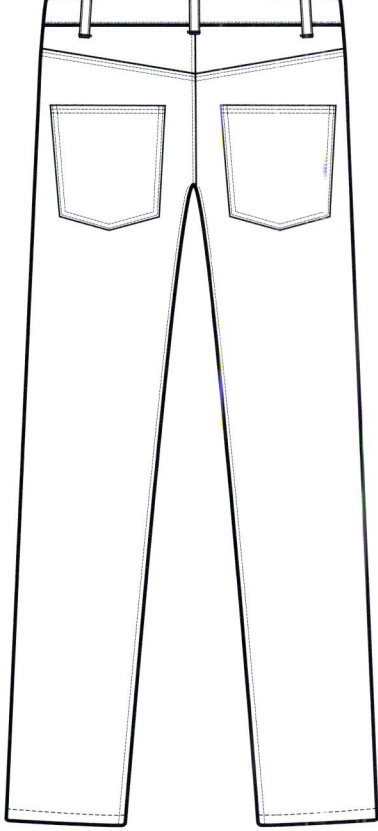

Pick large pockets with a straight shape. Place the pockets low, starting mid-butt or lower, and let them extend so that they also cover a part of the upper thigh.

TIP: This process can be tricky to figure out on your own so don't hesitate to ask someone you trust for some advice and pinning help.

RESULT
NARROWER BUTT

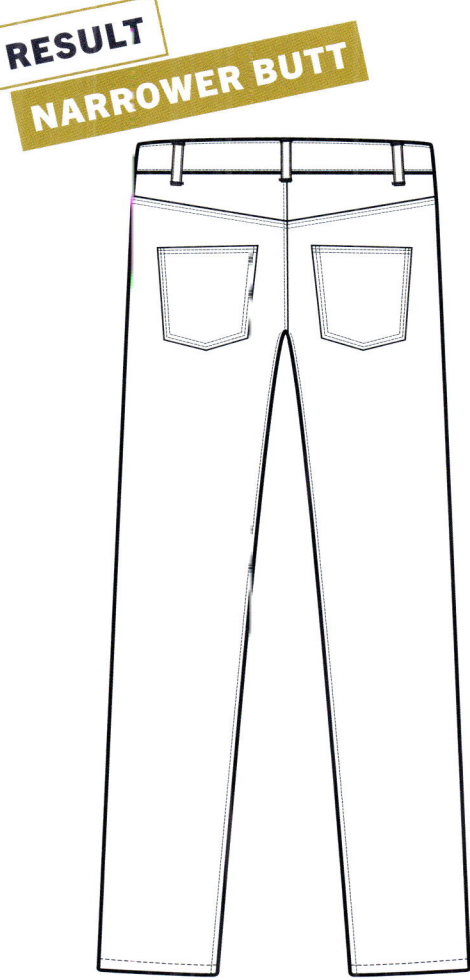

To make a wide butt look more narrow, move the pockets closer and place them on the center of your butt. A mid-size pocket is recommended.

BACK POCKET STITCHING

Originally referred to as the arcuate, the decorative stitching on back pockets has long been an essential trademark for many denim brands. Traditionally the arcuate was sewn on a double-needle machine for that iconic parallel stitching that brands like Levi's, Lee and Wrangler still use. Nowadays many motifs have a more freehand look that can easily be re-created on a home sewing machine.

THREAD AND STITCH OPTIONS

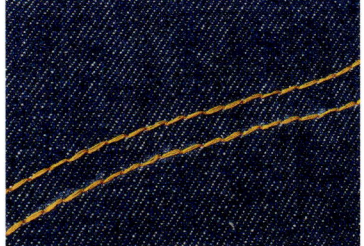

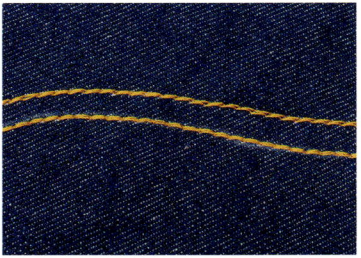

HEAVY THREAD
Use topstitching thread in the needle and regular sewing machine thread in the bobbin. Increase the stitch length to approximately 4–5 mm.

MULTIPLE THREADS
Wind two to three bobbins with regular sewing machine thread. Stack the bobbins on the spool pin. Thread as usual, then insert all the strands in the needle.
TIP: Use a topstitching needle with a larger eye to easily fit all the threads.

DOUBLE ROWS
Stitch a second row very close to the first row of stitching, using topstitching thread in the needle. This creates a subtle 3D effect that elevates the stitching. Make the stitching as parallel as possible for an even result.

FREEHAND STITCHING

> **SUPPLIES**
> - White tracing paper
> - Tracing wheel
> - Stitch design printed on regular office paper

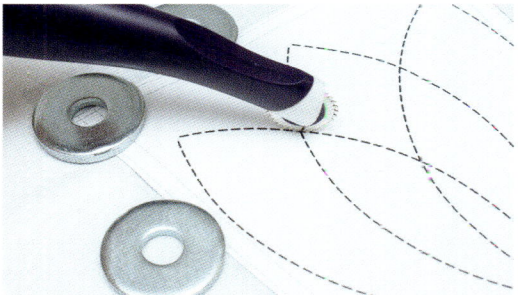

1 **Lay the tracing paper on the right side of the pocket.** Place the pocket design on top, and trace the entire pattern with a tracing wheel

2 **Stitch the pattern.** Sew slowly and be focused. Use your hands to gently guide the fabric so that the needle is always hitting the right spot. Always keep the needle down in the fabric when pivoting.

3 **Secure the stitch.** Depending on the design, overlap or backstitch to secure. To avoid bulk, rather than backstitching, decrease the stitch length for the last few stitches to secure the seam.

4 **The finished design.** Don't press the pocket until the tracing residue is removed with a damp cloth because heat will set the markings and make them hard to get rid of. Then proceed to press in the edges of the pocket following the method shown in *Back pockets* (pages 111–113).

PARALLEL STITCHING

SUPPLIES

- Stitch design printed on regular office paper
- Marking pencil, tailor's chalk or a chalk marking wheel

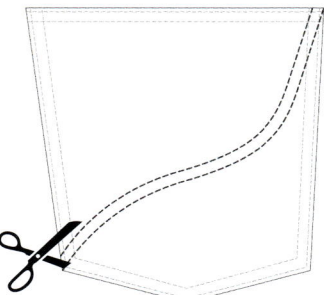

1 **Prepare the stencil.** Cut along the lines of the first row. The second row needs no marking because that will be stitched parallel to the first row using the edges of the presser foot as a guide.

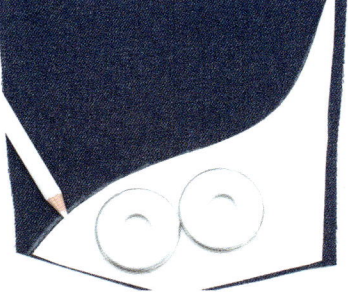

2 **Mark the first row of stitches.** Place the trimmed stencil on the right side of the back pocket. Draw along the edge using a marker.

3 **Prepare for stitching.** Always start at the edge of the fabric when stitching a traditional arcuate. With the needle in the fabric and threads pulled back, start stitching along the marked line.

4 **Pivot at the end.** The entire arcuate will be stitched in one sequence. When you reach the end of the first row, pivot with the needle in the fabric, and stitch along the edge until you reach the distance for the second row.

5 **Stitch the second row.** Using the edge of the presser foot as your seam guide, stitch a parallel row. The distance between the two rows should be approximately 6 mm (¼").

6 **Pivot to secure.** For a durable stitch, finish by stitching along the edge, and then over ap the first row for a few stitches, using a shorter stitch length. This is enough because the stitching will be even more secure once the pockets are topstitched in place on the jeans.

7 **The finished design.** Notice how the stitch is done as one continuous seam. Remove the tracing residue with a damp cloth before pressing in the edges of the pocket because heat can make the markings permanent.

CROTCH, YOKE AND SIDE SEAMS

The assembly of a pair of jeans is very different from the usual way of sewing together the legs of a pair of pants. The one downside of using the jeans method is that it's very hard to fit the jeans as you sew, so make sure that they fit properly before you start sewing the side seams.

SUPPLIES

- Topstitching thread and regular thread for the bobbin
- Regular sewing machine thread for sewing the pieces together
- Serger or a sewing machine for overcasting the fabric edges
- Edge presser foot for topstitching (optional)
- Jeans needle and topstitching needle (optional)

A PRIMER ON OVERCASTING

- **FOR SEAMS THAT ARE BEING TOPSTITCHED:** Overcast both layers after the seams have been sewn to save time and avoid bulk (e.g., the crotch and yoke seams).
- **FOR SEAMS BEING PRESSED APART:** Overcast each layer separately before you stitch the seam together (usually the outseam).
- **OVERCASTING ON A SERGER:** Use the wide 3-thread overlock or the 2-thread flatlock seam.
- **OVERCASTING ON A SEWING MACHINE:** A slightly wider zigzag stitch will work nicely.
- **SELVEDGE:** No overcasting needed.

TOPSTITCHING SIDE SEAMS

- For ease of construction, you need to choose between topstitching the outer or the inseam. For some inspiration, here is how some denim brands are doing it (though it might vary between styles too):
- **TOPSTITCHED INSEAM:** Lee, Levi's, Nudie Jeans, True Religion, Calvin Klein, Evisu
- **TOPSTITCHED OUTSEAM:** Wrangler

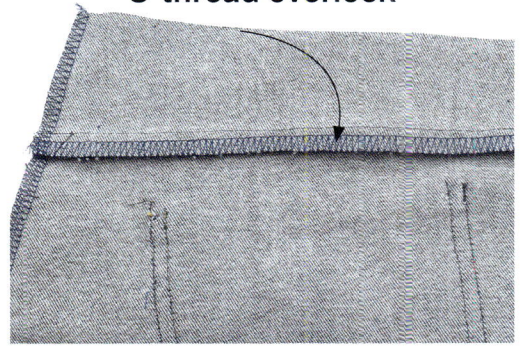

Straight stitch and 3-thread overlock

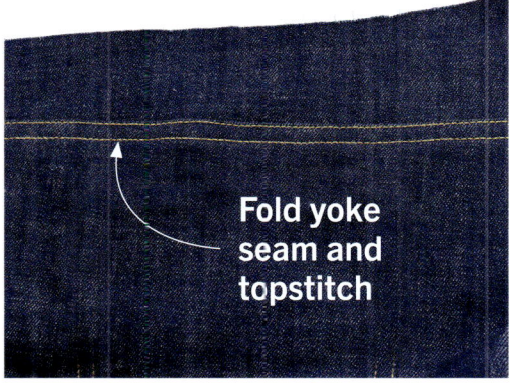

Fold yoke seam and topstitch

1 **Sew together the yoke and back leg piece.** Stitch and overcast each yoke separately before sewing the crotch seam. Use a 3-thread serger overlock or zigzag stitch to overcast the edge.

2 **Topstitch the yoke seam.** Fold the seam allowance downward or upward and topstitch two or three rows. See page 126–127 for more detailed instructions on how to topstitch the crotch.

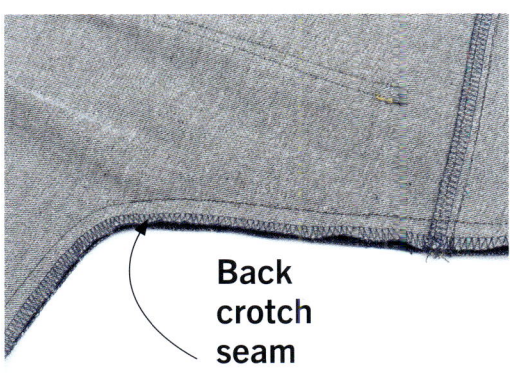

Back crotch seam

Seam allowance to the left

3 **Sew the crotch seam.** Lay the back pieces together, right sides facing, and sew the crotch seam using a regular straight stitch. Overcast the seam if you haven't done it already.

4 **Topstitch the crotch seam.** Fold the seam allowance to the left-hand side (with right side facing up), and topstitch the crotch seam (see pages 127–128 for detailed instructions). Then it's time to add the back pockets, if you haven't done these already (see page 110 for how to sew back pockets).

CROTCH, YOKE AND SIDE SEAMS

YOKE AND SIDE SEAMS

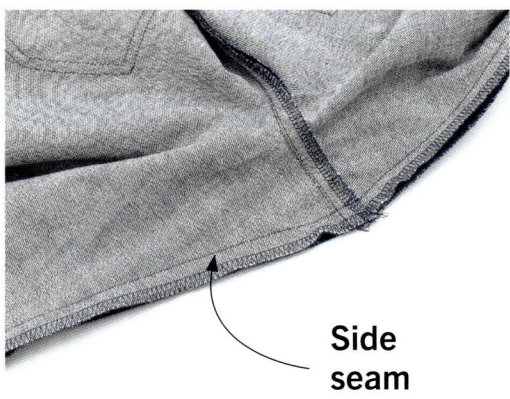

Side seam

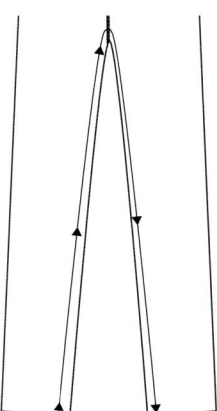

5 **Sew the side seam that you intend to topstitch.** In this tutorial, it's the inseam, but you can also topstitch the outseam.

6 **Inseam sewing order.** Sew from one leg opening to the other in one continuous seam, over the crotch, and don't stop until you have reached the other foot opening.

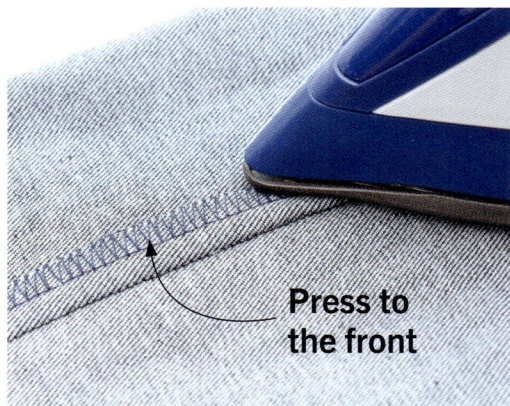

Press to the front

7 **Prepare for topstitching.** Fold the seam allowance towards the front (this is the standard direction for jeans inseams).

8 **Topstitch the inseam.** Stitch one or two rows all the way from one leg opening to the other one. **TIP:** Use a hump-jumper over the crotch seam area if you are experiencing problems with the feeding or getting skipped stitches.

9 **The inside of the seam.** For best result always use regular sewing machine thread in the bobbin when topstitching as thick thread might jam up in the bobbin.

10 **Sew the outseam.** Sew together both the seams using a straight stitch.

11 **Press apart the seam allowance.** If the outseam is not topstitched, the seam allowance is generally pressed open.

12 **Topstitch over the pocket area.** Fold the pocket seam allowance to the back. Stitch over the outseam on the back piece, close to the seam, and secure the seam properly. This is to reinforce the pocket area. Finish with a bar tack at the bottom of the stitch.

CROTCH, YOKE AND SIDE SEAMS

FLAT-FELLED YOKE AND CROTCH

For a professional look on your home-sewn jeans, you can flat-fell the yoke and crotch seam. This folding technique hides the raw edges and requires no overcasting. The drawback is that this seam is more difficult to sew than a regular topstitched seam, especially on curved areas.

BEFORE YOU START

This tutorial only shows the specific steps for stitching the yoke and back crotch. For instructions on how to adapt the pattern and prepare the seams, see *Sewing flat-felled seams* on pages 56–63.

If the flat-felled yoke seam will be pressed upwards, add the extra seam allowance to the yoke. For a yoke seam that is pressed downwards add the additional allowance to the upper leg piece.

SUPPLIES

- Topstitching or jeans sewing machine needle
- Sewing machine thread
- Heavy thread in the needle for the topstitching
- A hump-jumper
- A rubber mallet
- Measuring tape

1 **Prepare the yoke for topstitching.** Mark and fold the flat-felled seam according to the instructions on pages 58–59. Measure the size of the fold on several spots to ensure that the seam is folded evenly. This is especially important on curved areas because they can easily be misaligned.

2 **Topstitch the row closest to the edge.** Stitch a couple of millimetres in from the edge to close the folded seam. **TIP:** An edge guide foot will make it easier to stitch an even line along the folded edge.

3 **Topstitch the inner row.** Using a regular or topstitch presser foot, stitch the second row around 6 mm (¼") from the first row.
TIP: Use the outer edge of the presser foot toe as a seam guide, because that distance is usually around 5–6 mm.

4 **Fold and press the crotch seam.** Use the *Proper flat-felled seam* instructions on pages 58–59 for how to fold. Check from the right side that the left and right yoke stitching aligns perfectly. Pin or baste to keep the fold in place.

5 **Hammer down the crotch and yoke seam intersection (optional).** This area will be very bulky on flat-felled seams, especially on heavier denim, which makes it hard to topstitch. To reduce thickness, flatten the area with a rubber mallet.

Height tool

6 **Start topstitching the first row on the back crotch.** Beginning from the yoke, stitch along the edge. As soon as the area starts to tilt, insert a height compensation tool (hump-jumper) underneath the presser foot to keep it horizontal. If you don't do this, the stitching will likely be uneven, and you also run the risk of getting skipped stitches.

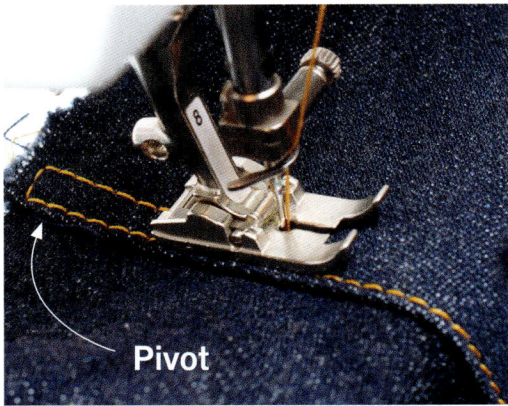

Pivot

7 **Insert the height compensation tool underneath the front of the presser foot if needed.** When the presser foot starts to point downwards, insert the height compensation tool. Gradually move the tool until the presser foot is level with the fabric again, then remove the tool.

8 **Stitch the second row without stopping.** Pivot at the end of the crotch and keep stitching as one long continuous sequence. Since this seam is so bulky, it's better to use a regular or topstitching foot for this step because an edge guide foot can make it harder to sew over the yoke bump.

9 **The finished flat-felled yoke and crotch seam.** This sequence was done on a regular domestic sewing machine with no special tools. The trick is to flatten the intersection bump and use a height compensation tool to keep the foot level.

10 **The reverse side.** Regular sewing machine thread is used in the bobbin to avoid tension issues and to ensure that the thread runs smoothly through the bobbin. The flat-felling is slightly uneven where the crotch and yoke intersect, which is hard to avoid entirely due to all the folded layers.

RECTANGULAR WAISTBAND

A rectangular waistband is the most common waistband style on jeans. Using separate inner and outer waistband pieces is recommended because the extra seam allowance will give the waistband more stability and shape. But you can also use a single waistband piece instead and fold it in the middle.

SUPPLIES

- Fusible interfacing
- Topstitching thread for the needle
- Sewing machine thread in the bobbin
- Jeans or topstitching needles
- Basting thread or washable double-sided tape

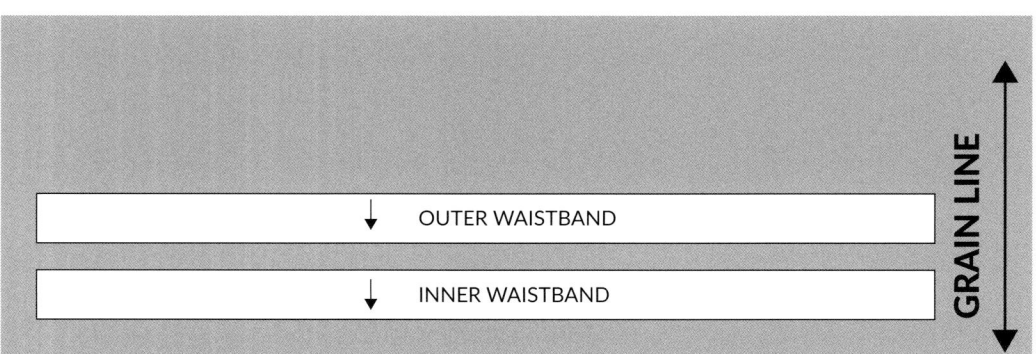

CUTTING THE WAISTBAND

Cut the waistband crosswise for more stretch and less shrinkage. Because woven fabric often shrinks more lengthwise and can keep shrinking after the first wash, a waistband cut along the grain will often shrink when washed, especially if the fabric hasn't been pre-washed several times.

Another advantage of cutting the waistband crosswise is that it will stretch out somewhat to fit your body when worn. A tip is to make the waistband slightly longer than needed and to trim away the surplus while sewing. This allows for more flexibility when sewing and fitting the waistband.

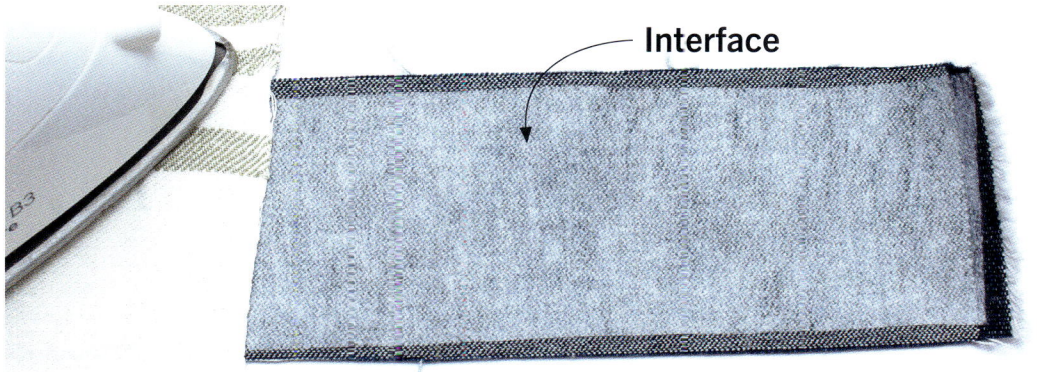

Interface

1 **Interface the waistband.** Cut a strip of lightweight interfacing slightly less wide than the waistband piece. Fuse according to the instructions of your chosen interfacing. While facing is not necessary, it does allow for more stability and control and can make the waistband easier to sew, especially if using stretch denim, easier to sew. If you are using heavy denim, you can omit the interfacing. On thinner or very stretchy denim, it's often best to interface both the inner and outer piece.

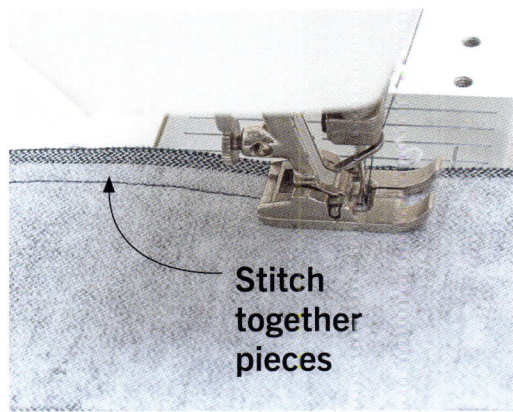

Stitch together pieces

2 **Sew together the outer and inner waistband.** Right sides are facing, the wrong side up. The seam allowance should be approximately 10 mm (⅜") wide.

3 **Press the seam.** First press the seam open. Then fold the pieces together and press again.

WAISTBAND

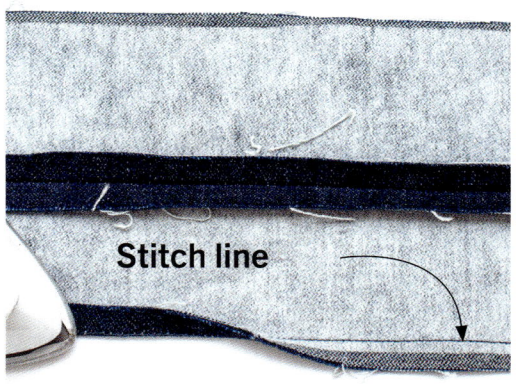

4 **Fold and press the inner seam allowance.** To make this easier, before folding, sew a straight stitch to mark the folding line, and use that as your guide.

5 **Attach the outer waistband.** Place the outer waistband on the jeans, right sides facing with the wrong side facing up.

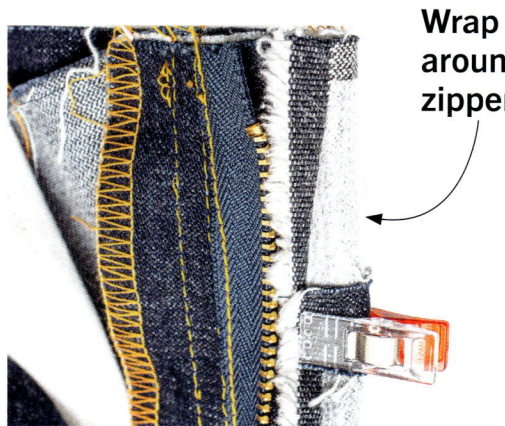

6 **Enclose the zipper fly.** Wrap 10–15 mm (3/8–5/8") of waistband fabric around the edge to encase the zipper fly. Pin or use clips to keep the waistband in place.

7 **End at the fly shield.** Do not trim or enclose the extra fabric yet; instead, wait to enclose the edge until you have begun sewing the waistband. This will give you more flexibility to fit as you sew.

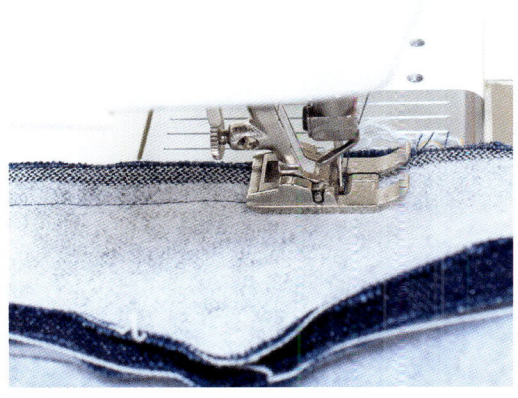

Wrap around shield

8 **Sew the waistband.** Starting at the zipper fly, stitch approximately 10 mm (⅜") from the edge.

9 **Enclose the end of the fly shield.** With approximately 25 mm (1") left, stop, but keep the needle in the fabric. Wrap the excess waistband fabric around the shield to encase the edge. Trim the fabric down to approximately 12 mm (½") and sew the remaining seam. Also, secure the top waistband seam again to prevent unravelling due to the trimming.

Fold in waistband edges

10 **Press in the seam allowances.** This method creates very crisp corners. The waistband will be enclosed with just topstitching rather than sewing together the ends of the waistband.

11 **Fold over the waistband.** Make sure all the pressed seam allowances are facing inwards in preparation for the topstitching.

WAISTBAND

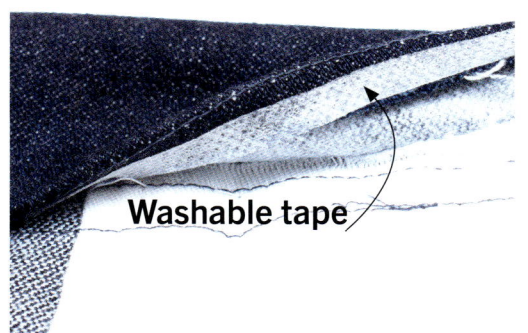

Washable tape

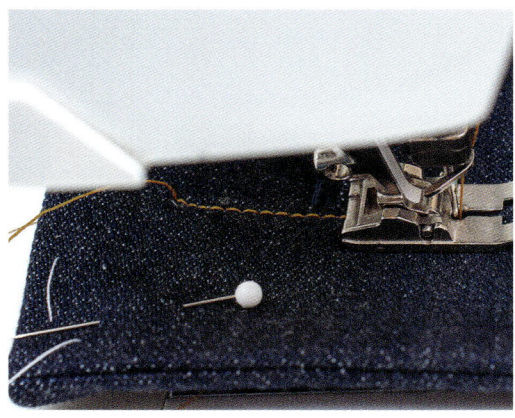

12 **Use double-sided washable tape or basting to keep the waistband in place.** This is optional but can help prevent the inner waistband from slipping or dragging when topstitched.

13 **Topstitch the waistband.** Start at the fly shield just after the bulky folded area to ensure that the presser foot lies flat. Stitch along the lower edge, making sure the stitch catches the inner waistband as well. **TIP:** Place your fingers underneath the waistband to guide the fold so that it aligns with the top layer.

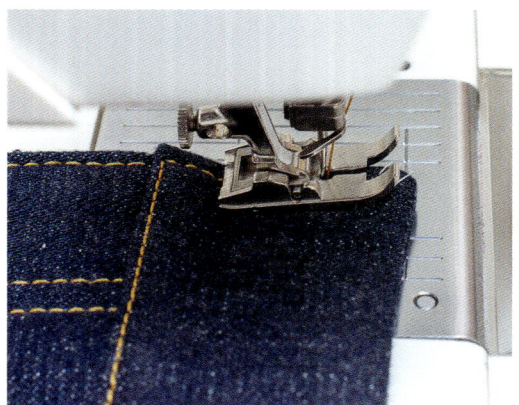

14 **Pivot at the zipper fly edge.** Continue stitching along the end of the waistband and upper edge.

15 **Level the presser foot for even feeding.** The sewing machine can have trouble sewing over the bulky areas, especially where several seams intersect. Insert a hump-jumper or another flat tool underneath the presser foot so that it stays horizontal, which helps with the feeding.

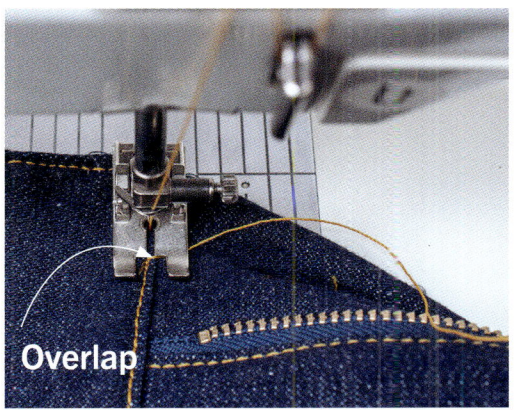

16 **Finish the seam.** Secure the topstitching. Instead of backstitching and to reduce bulk, decrease the stitch length when overlapping the topstitching. This secures the stitch without the need for backstitching.

17 **The finished waistband.** Sewing waistbands gets easier with practice, so don't worry if your first waistband doesn't look the way you had hoped. After a few tries, and by following the techniques and tips described in this tutorial, you'll see massive improvements.

18 **The inside of the waistband.** Regular sewing machine thread is used in the bobbin to ensure a balanced tension.
TIP: If you are having trouble getting the stitch to look even on the inside, use dark blue thread in the bobbin rather than a golden one to hide any irregular stitching.

SEWING A CURVED WAISTBAND

A curved waistband is contoured with a tapered fit on top, which fits better on some bodies compared to a straight waistband. The slight bias-cut also gives the waistband some built-in stretch. You can draft a curved waistband by following the instructions on pages 30–31 if your pattern lacks this option.

SUPPLIES

- Fusible interfacing
- Topstitching thread for the needle
- Sewing machine thread in the bobbin
- Jeans or topstitching needles
- Basting thread or washable double-sided tape
- Quilting ruler (optional)

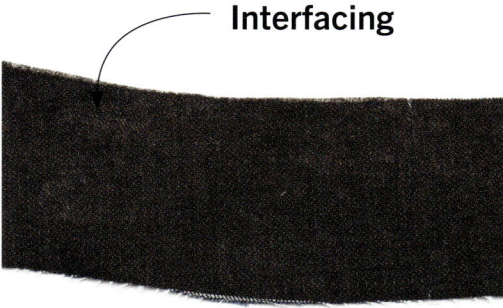

Interfacing

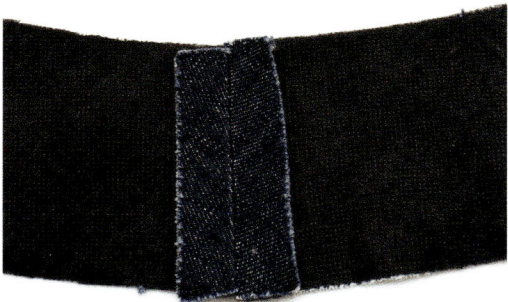

1 **Interface the waistband.** Either only interface the inner waistband piece, or for more stability, do it on both the inner and outer waistband pieces. Use a fairly lightweight fusible with some give because a curved waistband should have a little stretch for optimal comfort.

2 **Sew together the side seams if the waistband consists of several pieces.** Press the seams open.

3 **Stitch the outer and inner waistband together.** Use a narrow seam allowance, ideally no wider than 10–12 mm (⅜–½") because a narrow seam allowance helps the curve to shape without having to cut notches in the seam allowance.

4 **Press the waistband seam.** First press the seam open to flatten it. Then fold the pieces together and press again to shape the waistband.

5 **Stitch a folding line on the lower edge of the inner waistband.** This step will make folding the inner waistband easier when topstitching. Sew a straight stitch to mark the folding line using the same seam allowance or a few mm less so that the inner waistband edge extends slightly on the inside.
TIP: Use a quilting ruler in the ditch of the waistband seam to ensure a consistent waistband width. This is especially helpful if your waistband has some width variations, which is common when cutting a curved pattern on bias.

WAISTBAND

6 **Fold and press in the seam allowance on the inner waistband.** Use the stitch line as your guide for the fold.

7 **Double-check the width of the waistband.** Make sure the width is consistent around the entire waistband after the seam allowance is folded and pressed. If needed, adjust the width by folding the fabric less or more.

Wrap edges around zipper and shield

8 **Attach the outer waistband.** Place the outer waistband on the jeans, right sides facing with the wrong side up. Use pins or clips to keep the waistband in place.

9 **Enclose the zipper fly and fly shield.** Wrap the seam allowance around the edges of the waistband to encase the zipper fly and shield. Pin or use clips, making sure the fold fits snugly around the zipper. See *Rectangular waistband* on page 132 for more detailed instructions.

Fold in waistband edges

10 **Sew the waistband.** Starting at the zipper fly, stitch along the edge using your chosen seam allowance. Sew until you reach the end of the fly shield. Make sure the folds that are wrapping the edges stay snug and don't slip. See page 133 for more info on how to sew this step.

11 **Press in the seam allowances.** The waistband will be enclosed with just topstitching. There is no need to sew together the ends of the waistband before topstitching.

Washable tape

12 **Fold over the waistband.** Make sure all the pressed seam allowances are facing inwards in preparation for the topstitching. Press gently with an iron to ensure the folds stay in place.

13 **Use basting, double-sided washable tape or a glue stick to keep the fold in place.** This is optional but can help prevent the inner waistband from slipping or dragging when topstitched.

14 **Topstitch the waistband.** Start at the lower edge of the fly shield. Stitch using the method described in the *Rectangular waistband* section on pages 134–135 (steps 13–16).

15 **The finished waistband.** A curved waistband is harder to sew, due to both its shape and tendency to stretch out while sewing. But the method shown here helps to minimise those issues.

16 **Inside the waistband.** For a decorative effect, you can use a different fabric for the inner piece. Also, notice the blue thread in the bobbin. This is an easy way to make uneven topstitching less conspicuous.

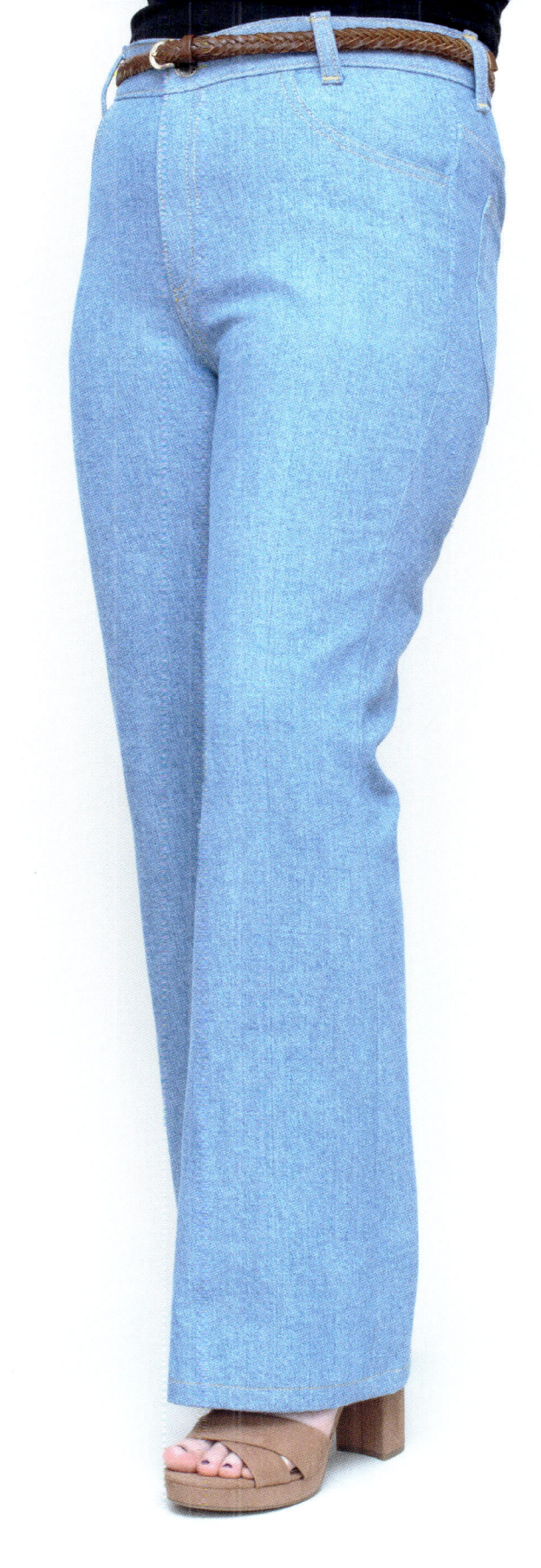

TRIPLE-LAYER BELT LOOPS

Perhaps the most popular method for home sewists, especially among those who also have a serger. The edges of the belt loop are overcast, then folded two times so that the finished width is one-third of the cut strip. To close the loop, the edges are topstitched on a sewing machine.

> **SUPPLIES**
> - Sewing machine
> - Edge presser foot (optional)
> - Serger (optional)
> - Press template (optional)
> - Topstitching thread in the needle
> - Sewing machine thread in the bobbin
> - Denim needle or a topstitching needle

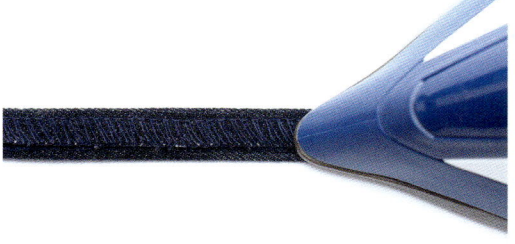

1 Cut and overcast the denim fabric strip. The strip should be three times (3X) the finished width. Use a wide serger 3-thread overlock or a sewing machine zigzag or overlock stitch to cover the edges.

2 Fold and press the belt loop strip. To make this easier use a paper press template the same width as the finished belt loop (see pages 150–151). Fold one-third of the strip, press and then fold a second time over the edge.

3 **Set up the machine.** Use topstitching thread in the needle and regular sewing machine thread in the bobbin. An edge guide presser foot makes it easier to sew straight but is not necessary. Begin by stitching the side with the overcasted outer layer; this will ensure the edge is properly secured.

4 **Start sewing.** Make sure the stitch catches the overcasted edge.

5 **Stitch the other edge.** Finish off by topstitching along the opposite side.

6 **The finished loop.** The main advantage of using this method is the flexibility it offers when it comes to size, thread options and the needles used. It will, however be more bulky than the versions sewn with a coverstitch or twin-needle (see upcoming pages).

TWIN-NEEDLE BELT LOOPS

Belt loops sewn with a twin-needle are a quick and easy option that can be sewn entirely on the sewing machine. For best results use a jeans twin-needle, but be aware that a twin-needle might not be sturdy enough for heavy denim fabrics. On the reverse side, a zigzag stitch is formed with visible loops from the needle thread.

You might need to experiment with the tension to get this stitch right. If there is a ridge forming between the straight stitches, try lowering the needle thread tension.

SUPPLIES

- Topstitching thread or regular sewing machine thread in the needles
- Regular sewing machine thread in the bobbin
- Denim twin-needle 100/16
- Bias tape maker or paper press template to fold the loops

1 Cut a fabric strip. The strip should be folded twice the width of the finished belt loop. The length of the piece should be as long as all the belt loops plus seam allowances. Don't overcast the edges; the zigzag stitch on the reverse side will keep the edges from fraying.

2 Fold and press the belt loops. Use a bias tape maker or a press template (pages 146–147) to fold the belt loop.

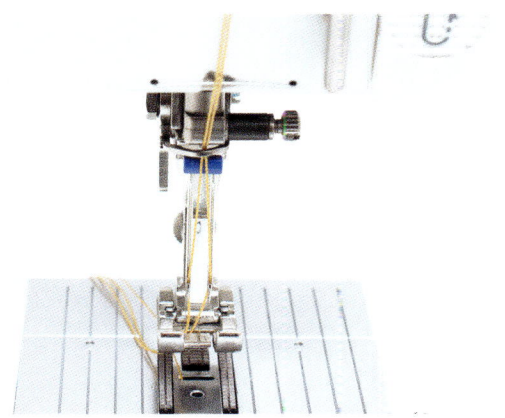

3 **Set up the machine.** Insert the twin-needle, and make sure it sits tightly in the slot. Thread the machine with two spools of needle thread (or stack two bobbins on the spool pin). Check your manual for the recommended settings for a twin-needle and increase the stitch length according to preference.

4 **Insert the folded loop in the sewing machine.** Make sure it's properly centred, using the presser foot as a guide.

5 **Start sewing.** Sew slowly, guiding the loop with your hands to make sure the seam stays centred.

6 **The finished belt loop.** This method is one of the fastest ways to sew belt loops on a domestic sewing machine. Don't fret over the zigzag stitches looking a bit uneven, with the needle thread loops showing on the reverse side; it's totally normal.

COVERSTITCH BELT LOOPS

In the garment industry, jeans belt loops are sewn on a coverstitch machine, using a folding attachment. But you can achieve a similar result using a piece of cardboard to create evenly folded loops.

SUPPLIES

- Regular sewing thread for the needles (most domestic coverstitch machines can't handle topstitch thread in the needles)
- Serger thread for the looper
- 2-needle wide coverstitch
- Size 90/14 needles
- A piece of cardboard

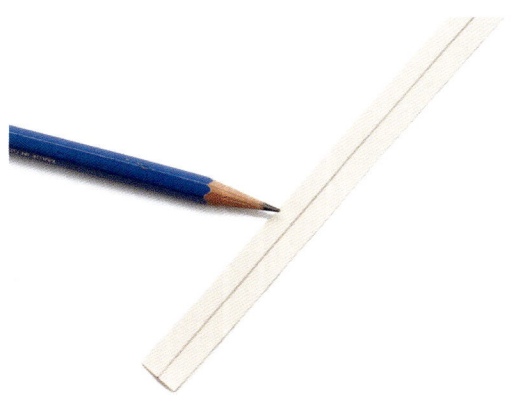

1 Cut a piece of cardboard. The width should be the same as the finished belt loops—around 12 mm (½") is a common width. The length of the piece should ideally be as long as all the belt loops plus seam allowances. Draw a line in the middle with a pencil.

2 Cut the belt loop strip. The fabric should be cut lengthwise. Cut a strip that is twice the finished width; you can add a few millimetres extra to compensate for the fold if the denim is thick.

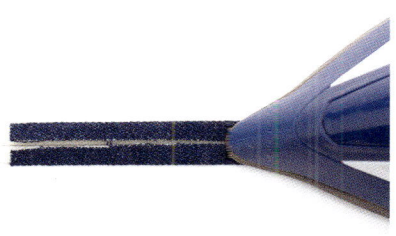 

3 **Fold the loop.** Align the fabric edges with the line on the cardboard. Press with an iron to shape the fabric around the cardboard strip. Remove the cardboard, and press again.

4 **Stitch the belt loops.** The needles should hit the fabric on the first stitch.

5 **Make sure you sew in the middle.** Use the edges of the presser foot as a guide. You can also use a separate seam guide or a piece of Lego attached with Blu Tack or easy-to-remove tape.

6 The finished loop.

COVERSTITCH BELT LOOPS WITH FOLDER

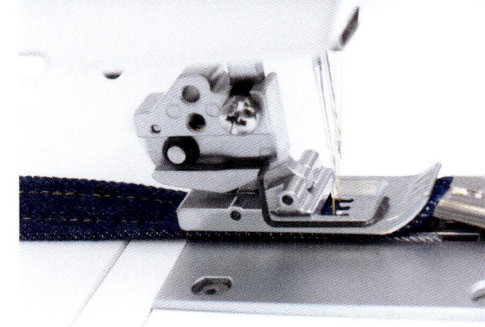

Using a belt loop folding attachment, you can make professional-looking belt loops in just a few minutes. Some coverstitch machine brands have this tool in their accessory range, but you can also use a generic folder and attach it onto the machine with tape.

SUPPLIES

- Belt loop folder
- Regular sewing thread for the needles (some domestic coverstitch machines can't handle topstitch thread in the needles)
- Serger thread for the looper
- 2-needle wide coverstitch
- Size 90/14 needles

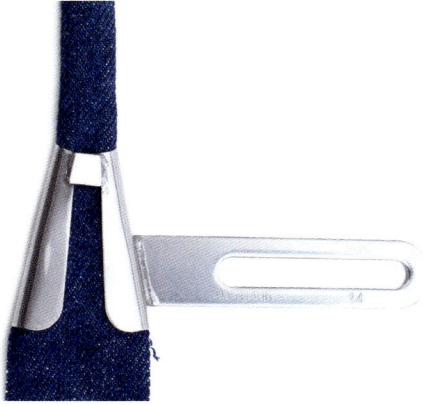

1 Cut the belt loop strip. The fabric should be cut along the grainline. Cut a strip that is twice the finished width. If the loop attachment has edges overlap, add the extra width according to the instructions.

2 Insert the strip into the folder. Pull out around 5 cm (2") so that the presser foot can fully grab the fabric when you are coverstitching.

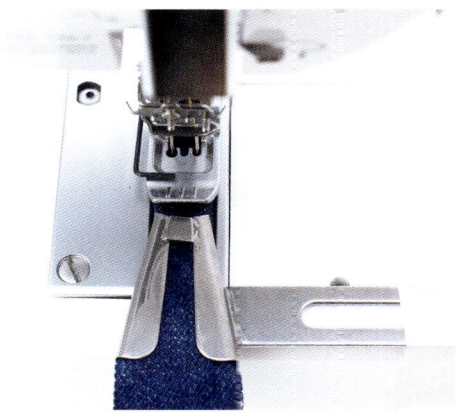 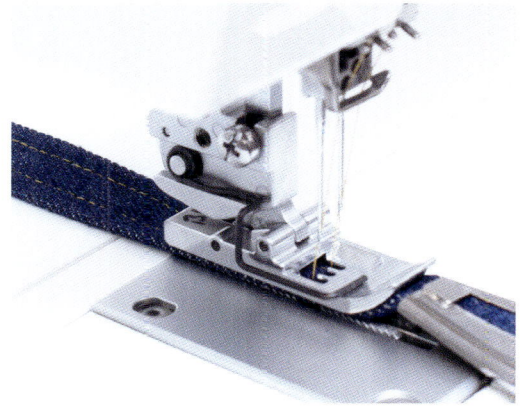

3 **Stitch the belt loop.** Attach the folder and insert the folded loop underneath the presser foot. The needles should hit the fabric on the first stitch.

4 **Make sure you stitch in the middle.** Move the folder slightly if needed.

5 **The finished belt loop string.** Cut the loop into pieces of equal length.

SINGLE STITCH BELT LOOP

Mostly used by niche designer denim brands, this unusual belt loop style is sewn together with only one stitch. There is no loop turning involved—just a single line of topstitching is needed to enclose the edges.

While it might look intriguing, the assembly method is actually quite straightforward. All you need to do is create a simple press template and then sew the belt loops with a regular sewing machine.

SUPPLIES

- Topstitching thread for the needle
- Sewing machine thread for the bobbin
- Denim or a topstitching needle
- Cardboard and pencil for the press template

1 **Cut a piece of cardboard.** The press template should be the same width as the finished belt loop. Draw a line one-third in with a pencil.

2 **Cut a denim strip.** The strip should be three times (3X) the finished width plus an additional 3 mm (⅛") extra to allow for the folding of the upper edge.

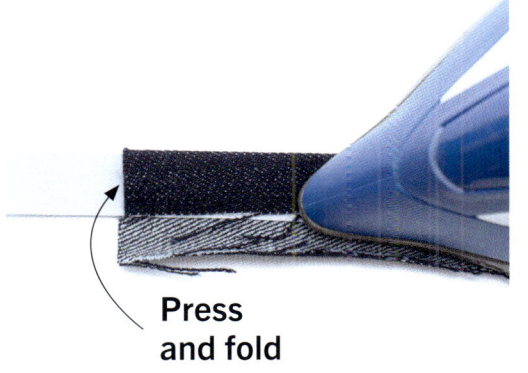

Press and fold

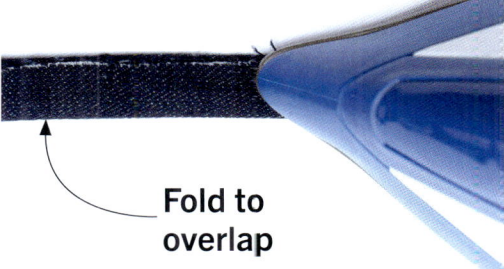

Fold to overlap

3 **Do the first fold.** Place the template inside the strip, fold and press the strip over the template so that the edges meet.

4 **Fold and press the opposite side over the template so that it overlaps.** The raw edge should extend to the edge of the template.

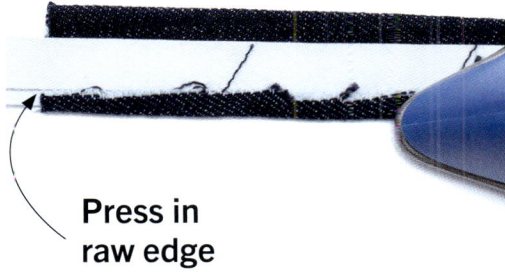

Press in raw edge

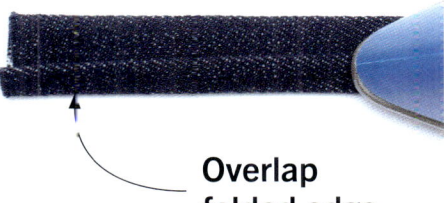

Overlap folded edge

5 **Open up the fold and press in the overlapping raw edge.** The upper edge should be pressed in so that it aligns with the drawn line, one-third in.

6 **Fold the opposite side (with the pressed-in edge) over the template.** The folded edge should extend slightly over the mid-point of the template.

 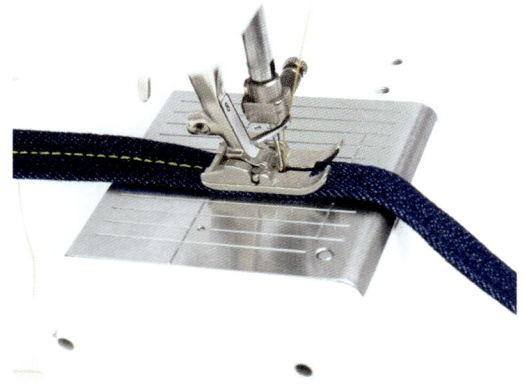

7 Set up the sewing machine. Use topstitching thread in the needle and regular sewing machine thread in the bobbin. A denim or topstitching needle is recommended. Insert the folded strip of fabric with the central fold on the underside.

8 Start sewing. The stitch should be in the middle of the loop. Use the edges of the presser foot as your guide to ensure the stitch is properly aligned. Use your index finger or middle finger to keep the fold in place on the underside of the belt loop strip.

9 The finished belt loop. While the prep work involves some extra steps, the actual sewing is quick, and the end result is a very unique look that is created with no special tools or machines.

ATTACHING BELT LOOPS

This method makes attaching belt loops easy and precise without any extra tools and is very similar to the assembly process used in the garment industry.

> **SUPPLIES**
> - Topstitching thread and regular thread for the bobbin
> - Denim or topstitching needle
> - A hump-jumper to level the presser foot

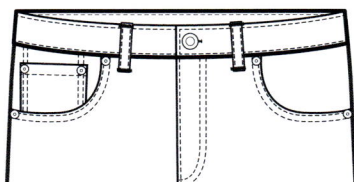 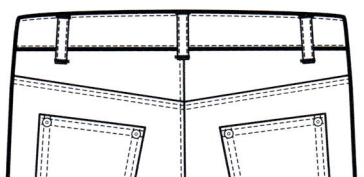

TIPS FOR SEWING BELT LOOPS ON JEANS

- Most jeans have five belt loops: mid-back, two on the sides of the back, around 3–5 cm (1½–2") from the side seam, and two just outside of the front pocket seam.

- Belt loops can be placed at the edge of the upper waistband or slightly below. The belt loops then usually extend at least around 2.5–3 cm (1–1¼") below the lower edge of the waistband.

- The most important consideration when sewing belt loops is that they are long enough to fit the belts you are intending to wear.

- Creating an X with two belt loops crossing each other at the mid-back seam is another option.

- If you are having problems stitching over all the layers, use a hump-jumper to level the presser foot.

- Try increasing the stitch length of the bar tacks to make the feeding smoother.

- Use heavy topstitching thread in the needle, but regular sewing machine thread in the bobbin. This will prevent the thread from getting jammed up.

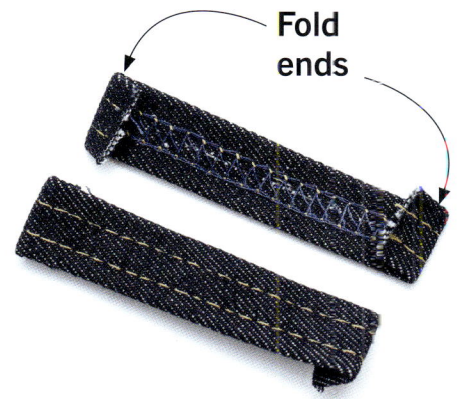

1 **Fold and press the ends of the belt loops.** The folds should be about 10–15 mm (⅜–⅝") wide. Press with an iron to set the folds. There is no need to overcast the edges; they won't unravel, and a slight fraying is part of the look on traditional denim belt loops.

2 **Attach the upper edge of the belt loop.** Sew a row of straight stitching in the ridge of the upper fold. Back stitch to secure.
TIP: Use a pin or a dab of basting glue or glue stick to keep the loop in place if it is slipping.

3 **Topstitch along lower edge.** Use a narrow zigzag stitch with a shorter stitch length. Backstitch at the start and the end. For extra security let the stitch extend just outside the edge of the belt loop.
TIP: For a more artisan look, use irregular rows of straight stitches instead to attach the loops.

4 **Topstitch over the upper edge.** Again, use a narrow zigzag stitch with a shorter stitch length, and stitch a few millimetres in from the folded edge.

BELT LOOPS INSIDE THE WAISTBAND

Enclosing one end of a belt loop inside the waistband is a technique used by many denim brands. It's actually very easy to do and provides a very neat finish. Just make sure to add extra length because the loops need to be around 25 mm (1") longer than regular belt loops.

SUPPLIES

- Topstitching thread
- Regular sewing machine thread
- Denim or topstitching needle
- A hump-jumper to level the presser foot
- Measuring tape

1 **Stitch the belt loops to the upper edge.** This step is done before attaching the waistband. Use a straight stitch, and sew close to the edge. For suggestions on belt loops placement, see page 154.

2 **Sew the waistband.** Attach the waistband; see *Rectangular waistband* on page 130 for sewing instructions. Make sure the loops don't get skewed diagonally when sewn over. Pinning the loops can help them stay vertical.

3 **Use a tool to level the foot.** The belt loops add even more bulk, which can cause problems when topstitching, especially over the back crotch seam. Insert a hump-jumper tool to keep the foot horizontal.

4 **Measure the fold placement.** It's entirely up to personal preference how far down the fold should be, but a good ballpark is around 25 mm (1"). The most important thing is that the loops are long enough to fit a belt.

5 **Stitch the fold.** Use regular sewing machine thread for this step because it will reduce the bulk. This stitch will keep the loops in place when they are they are stitched over with bar tacks.

BELT LOOPS

6 **After attaching the waistband, fold and press the upper edge.** The fold should align with the edge of the waistband. Around 10 mm (⅜") is a good fold width, but a wider one is fine too, because you can always trim the extra strip afterwards.

7 **Stitch the upper belt loop.** Use the bar tack techniques described on pages 64–65 and make sure the stitch is secured properly. Use regular thread in the bobbin, and increase the stitch length if the machine won't feed the fabric evenly.

8 **Stitch the lower edge.** Use the same bar tack technique as on the upper edge.

9 **The finished belt loop.** Trim away any extra fabric inside the top loop fold so that the fold allowance is no more than 10 mm (⅜"). This method creates a very elegant finish and is almost as quick to sew as the regular jeans belt loop attachment method.

RIVETS

Rivets are traditionally used to reinforce high-stress seams such as the pocket areas. But they are also a decorative feature that come in many different metallic finishes and designs.

> **SUPPLIES**
> - Rivets and nails
> - An awl, punch pliers or other punching tools for making the holes
> - A hammer, a pair of pliers, an anvil or a hand-press machine to attach the rivets
> - A die or tool set to ensure a more precise application (optional, but recommended)

1 **Mark the rivet placing.** Don't place it too close to the seam edge; there needs to be room for the entire rivet once installed.

2 **Pierce a hole.** Using an awl, a hammer plus a puncher tool or a sturdy pair of pliers, punch a small hole through the denim layers.

3 **Push the nail through the hole from the reverse side.** Make sure it is firmly pressed all the way up.

4 **Trim the nail if needed.** If the fabric is thin, the nail might be too long. If so, cut away the surplus tip using a sturdy wire cutter. This should be done after you've inserted the nail into the fabric because the cutter might squeeze and blunt the tip.

5 **Place the top rivet on top.** Do this from the right side. Make sure the rivet sits properly on the nail.

6 **Prepare the tools.** Ideally, you should use a set of dies or fastening tools that are made especially for the rivets that you plan to use. The lower part is used to keep the nail in place, and the top piece has an indent that will protect the rounded convex or concave top that many rivets have. If the rivet has a flat top, a special tool set isn't as necessary.

7 **Hammer down the rivet.** Do it carefully on the center of the rivet. Make sure you hammer straight; stop and check before entirely securing the rivet to the nail. This is especially important if you don't use a die or tool set for the rivets.

8 **Check the rivet.** Grab the rivet with your fingers and try wiggle it back and forth to make sure it sits firmly and doesn't move when touched. If needed, do some more light hammering to set the rivet fully.

SEWING BUTTONHOLES

The trick when sewing jeans buttonholes on a regular sewing machine is to use a longer stitch length, with regular sewing machine thread in the bobbin, and to sew the buttonhole using manual settings, not the automatic ones.

These precautions will prevent problems such as uneven feeding and jammed up thread.

SUPPLIES

- Topstitching thread and regular thread for the bobbin
- Marking pen
- Jeans or topstitching needles
- Buttonhole cutter or seam ripper
- Buttonhole presser foot (but a regular presser foot works too)

TIPS FOR SEWING JEANS BUTTONHOLES

- Increase the stitch length on the zigzag/buttonhole stitch. Heavy thread needs more space. If the stitch is too closely spaced, the sewing machine can't feed properly.

- Thick materials can also cause problems with the feeding. By increasing the stitch length, you will mitigate this issue.

- Don't use an automatic buttonhole presser foot for denim. It will not feed as well on heavy fabrics as a regular buttonhole presser foot does.

- Use heavy topstitching thread in the spool, but regular sewing machine thread in the bobbin. This will prevent the thread from getting jammed up.

- Use a topstitching needle for the best result. They have larger eyes and are designed to cut through thick materials.

RIVETS AND BUTTONS

1 **Mark the buttonhole.** Use tailor's chalk to mark the buttonhole opening. To figure out the right length of the button opening, calculate the diameter of the button plus the height plus the end tacks. Also, make the end tacks markings extra long, longer than the presser foot is wide because this makes the ends easier to gauge when sewing the buttonholes.

2 **Prepare the machine.** Use topstitching or buttonhole thread in the needle and regular thread in the bobbin. Insert a topstitch needle or a large denim needle. Increase the stitch length compared with your regular buttonhole settings.

3 **Sew a test sample.** Always do a sample buttonhole first to gauge the proper size of the opening and stitch settings. Ideally, the sample should also be interfaced so that it mimics the waistband properties.

4 **Sew the buttonhole.** Starting at the inner end, sew around and finish with end tacks, just like you would sew a regular buttonhole. If your machine has the option, try a keyhole buttonhole (pictured).

5 **Cut the buttonhole open.** Use a buttonhole cutter or a good quality seam ripper to open the buttonhole. The advantage of the cutter over the ripper is that it is sharper, which is helpful when cutting through thick denim.

6 **The finished buttonhole.** This method creates a durable yet easy to sew buttonhole.

FLAT TOP BUTTONS

This common denim button type is usually called flat top or tack button, referring to its flat surface, which is often embossed or engraved. You don't need any special tools to attach them—a regular hammer will do the job perfectly. Flat top buttons come in many different coatings, such as brass, copper, silver and even enamel.

SUPPLIES

- Denim button and nail (tack)
- Tailor's pen for marking
- Awl for making the hole
- Hammer to attach the button

1 **Mark the placement of the button.** Overlap the waistband so that it closes. With a pen or an awl, mark a dot around 3 mm (⅛") away from the end of the buttonhole.

2 **Pierce a hole.** Use an awl to pierce a hole so that the denim button can be attached with a nail from the reverse side.

3 **Insert the nail.** Push the nail through the hole from the reverse side of the waistband.

4 **Place the button on top.** From the right side, place the button over the nail. Make sure the button fits properly on the nail.

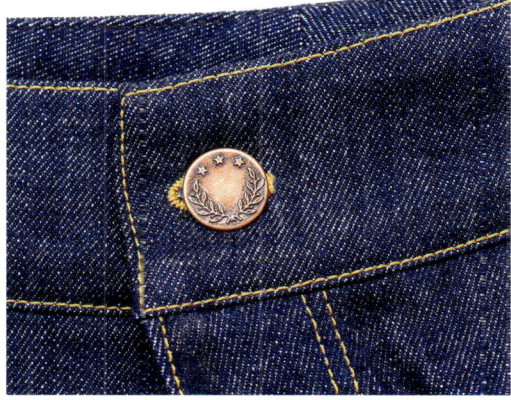

5 **Hammer down the button.** Turn wrong side up, keeping the button in place. Hit the nail with several fairly light punches. Make sure the hammer hits the middle of the nail. Keep hammering until the button is fully locked. Wiggle the button with your fingers to make sure it sits firmly. Hammer more if needed.

6 **The finished button.** This denim button style is called flat top. The embossed wreath design has been used on denim buttons since the early 20th century.

DONUT BUTTONS

Named after the donut-like opening in the center, this button style has been used on jeans for more than a century and is regarded by many as the most authentic button style for jeans.

The donut button is attached with a nail that needs to be pressed down. You can do this manually with an anvil, which is the method shown here. But you'll get a better result using a hand press machine because that tool smooths out the tip of the nail and creates a beautiful, round shape.

> **SUPPLIES**
> - Donut button and nail
> - An awl or punch pliers for making the holes
> - A hammer, a pair of pliers, an anvil or a hand-press machine to attach the rivets
> - A die or tool set to ensure a more precise application (optional)

1 Mark the placement. Overlap the waistband. With a pen or an awl, mark a dot very close to the outer end of the buttonhole.

2 Pierce a hole. Use an awl or a punching tool to pierce a hole. The hole only needs to be big enough for the nail to fit into.

3 **Insert the nail.** Push the nail through the hole from the reverse side of the waistband.

4 **Place the donut button on top.** From the right side, put the button over the nail.

5 **Hammer down the nail tip.** Place the waistband on a hard surface, with the button facing up. Hammer down the nail using an anvil. Make sure the hammer hits the middle of the nail. Stop and check every few hits. Keep hammering until the nail flattens and the button is locked, which can take quite a while when using handheld tools.

6 **The finished donut button.** It's tricky to get a perfectly shaped top in the middle when using a hammer and an anvil. A pressing machine will generally yield a better and quicker result, but with some practice, handheld tools can be sufficient.

STRAIGHT STITCH JEANS HEM

You can successfully hem a pair of jeans using a domestic sewing machine. The key is to use regular thread in the bobbin and a hump-jumper when hemming over the bulky side seams.

The only drawback with using a sewing machine straight stitch instead of a chainstitch is that it doesn't achieve the same roping effect, which refers to the subtle wave at the hem that one often sees on industrial-made jeans.

SUPPLIES

- Topstitching thread for the needle
- Regular sewing machine thread in the bobbin
- Topstitching or denim needles
- Hump-jumper to level the presser foot

PREPARATION

For less bulk, leave the hem raw, although you can also overcast the fabric edge using an overlock or zigzag stitch before hemming. Always do a sample on your chosen fabric before hemming to get the settings right. Experiment with the needle tension settings and stitch length to get the seam looking balanced.

If the tension is still off, try changing the bobbin tension as well. Remember to mark the original tension setting on the bobbin, or use a second bobbin for topstitching purposes.

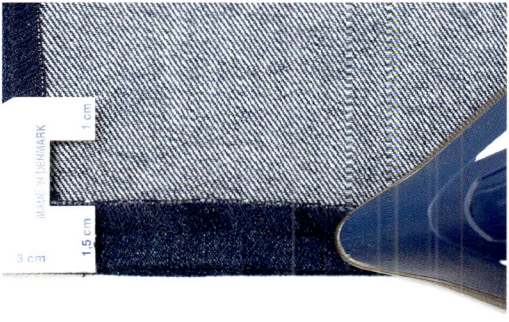 

1 **Fold and press the hem.** The standard finished jeans hem width is around 13–15 mm (⅝").

2 **Fold and press again.** Let the edge of the fabric be your guide when folding the second time; you don't need to measure the fold this time.

3 **Prepare the machine.** Use topstitching thread in the needle and regular sewing thread in the looper. Insert a topstitching or denim needle, make sure the needle sits firmly in the slot.

4 **Start sewing at the inner leg seam.** Start stitching along the leg hem, you don't need to backstitch at the beginning.

5 **Stitch close to the upper folded edge.** Placing your index finger inside the leg opening, at the tip of the fold, and then pinching the outside with your thumb makes sewing close to the edge easier.

6 **Use a hump-jumper when sewing over the side seams.** Place the tool underneath the presser foot to level the foot; this will ensure that the fabric is fed evenly and prevent skipped stitches.

7 **Finish the seam.** Backstitch or decrease the stitch length to secure the seam and snip the threads. You can also secure the thread by hand using the method shown on page 176.

8 **The finished hem.** You can also use dark navy thread in the bobbin to hide any seam irregularities on the inside hem.

CHAINSTITCHED JEANS HEM

The traditional way to hem jeans in the garment industry is to use a chainstitch machine. A chainstitch seam ages into a subtle wave at the hem that is called a roping effect, a signature feature on authentic jeans.

A similar look can be achieved on a domestic coverstitch machine, using the 1-needle chainstitch set-up. The drawback, however, is that a chainstitch is more prone to unravelling, so make sure to properly secure the seam.

> **SUPPLIES**
> - Regular sewing thread for the needles (some domestic coverstitch machines can't handle topstitch thread in the needles)
> - Serger, sewing machine thread or woolly polyester for the looper
> - 1-needle chainstitch set-up
> - Size 90/14 needle

PREPARATION

Sew together the side seams. Don't overcast the edge of the fabric—leave it raw. It will be less bulky, and it won't fray once the seam is folded and stitched.

Always do a sample on your chosen fabric before hemming to get the settings right. Experiment with changing the tension, decreasing the differential feed, and adjusting the presser foot pressure when sewing denim on a coverstitch machine.

HEMS

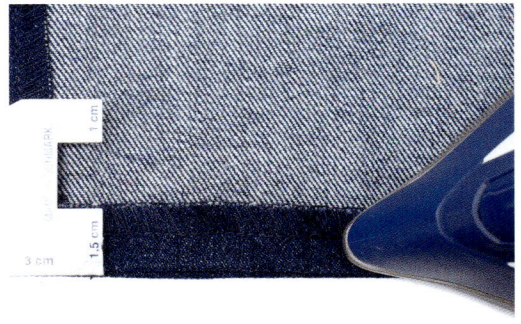

1 **Fold and press the hem.** The standard finished jeans hem width is around 13–15 mm (⅝").

2 **Fold and press again.** Let the edge of the fabric be your guide when folding the second time; you don't need to measure the fold this time.

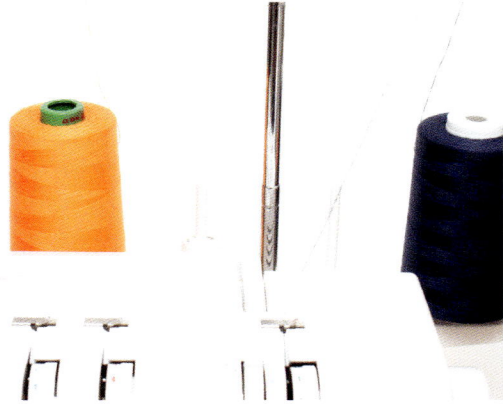

3 **Prepare the machine.** Use sewing thread in the needle and serger or regular sewing thread in the looper. The thread to the left in the picture is regular sewing machine thread that comes on cones. Use a size 90/14 needle and set your machine for single needle chainstitch.

4 **Start sewing just after the inseam.** Because a coverstitch machine is sensitive to bulk, don't start by sewing over a seam.

5 **Stitch close to the upper folded edge.** Make sure you feed the fabric evenly; don't tug it.

6 **Use a hump-jumper when sewing over the side seams.** Place the tool underneath the presser foot to level the foot; this will ensure that the fabric is fed evenly and prevent skipped stitches.

7 **Close the seam.** Let the chainstitch overlap for a few stitches.

8 **Remove the garment.** Release the threads, pinch the seam ends between your fingers and carefully remove the leg opening from the machine.

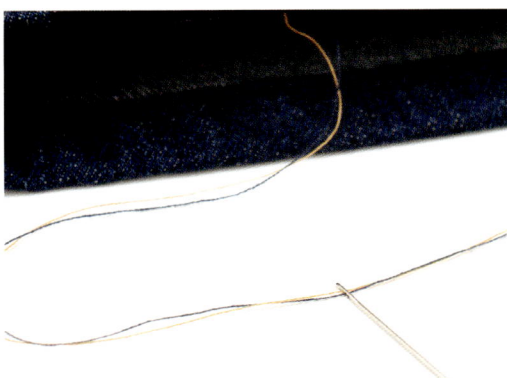

9 Prepare for securing the threads. Pull the needle thread to the reverse side using a sewing needle. Cut away the beginning thread; this does not need to be secured.

10 Insert the looper thread. Once the needle is on the reverse side, insert the end looper thread so that both the needle thread and looper thread is in the needle eye.

11 Secure the end threads. Tie the threads into a knot using the needle, and secure the knot by attaching it to the fabric. Cut the surplus thread.

12 The finished hem. As you can see, there is already a subtle wave on the inside of the leg opening. This is the signature look of jeans hemmed with a chainstitch, and it will become more pronounced over time.

TRIPLE STRAIGHT STITCH HEM

A triple straight stitch is a durable stitch sewn in a two steps forward, one step back sequence. Unlike a regular straight stitch, the triple version has stretch, which makes it a good choice for sewing a narrow hem on stretchy stovepipe jeans.

Because the thickness is achieved with a back and forth movement, there is no need for heavy topstitching thread, and in fact, a regular sewing machine thread is a better choice for the triple straight stitch. Also called 3-step security stitch or triple stretch stitch, it's found on most modern sewing machines.

SUPPLIES

- Regular sewing machine thread
- Denim or topstitch sewing machine needle

The symbol for triple straight stitch is usually three parallel dashed lines. Check the manual for the recommended stitch length and tension settings.

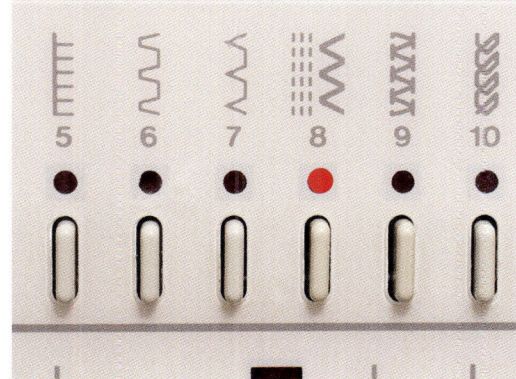

1 **Set the machine up.** Use regular sewing machine thread in the needle and bobbin. Some machine brands also recommend using a non-standard presser foot for this stitch. You can experiment with increasing the stitch length to make it look even more like traditional denim topstitching.

2 **Start sewing.** This stitch is slow to sew because of the back and forth movement, but resist the temptation to speed up or tug the fabric, this can distort the seam. To finish the seam, let it overlap for a few stitches. There is generally no need to go in reverse to secure this stitch since it is already sewing a reverse stitch in each sequence.

3 **The finished hem.** The thickness of the stitch combined with the stretch and durability makes this a great choice for stretch jeans, especially if you don't have a coverstitch and can't sew a chainstitch.

4 **The reverse side.** While the seam is not as neat on the reverse, it does resemble the reverse side of a chainstitch, so it could be an attractive option for hems that are meant to be turned up.

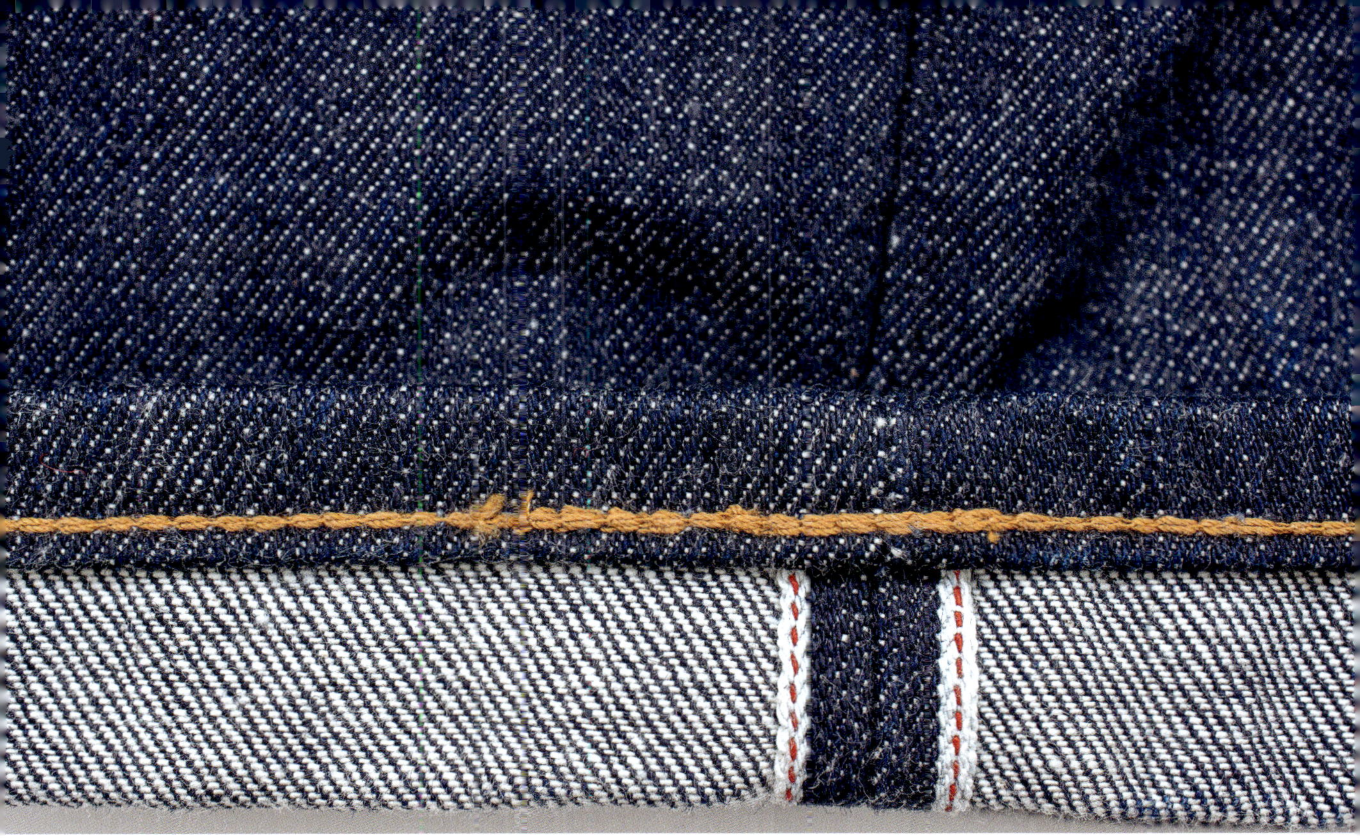
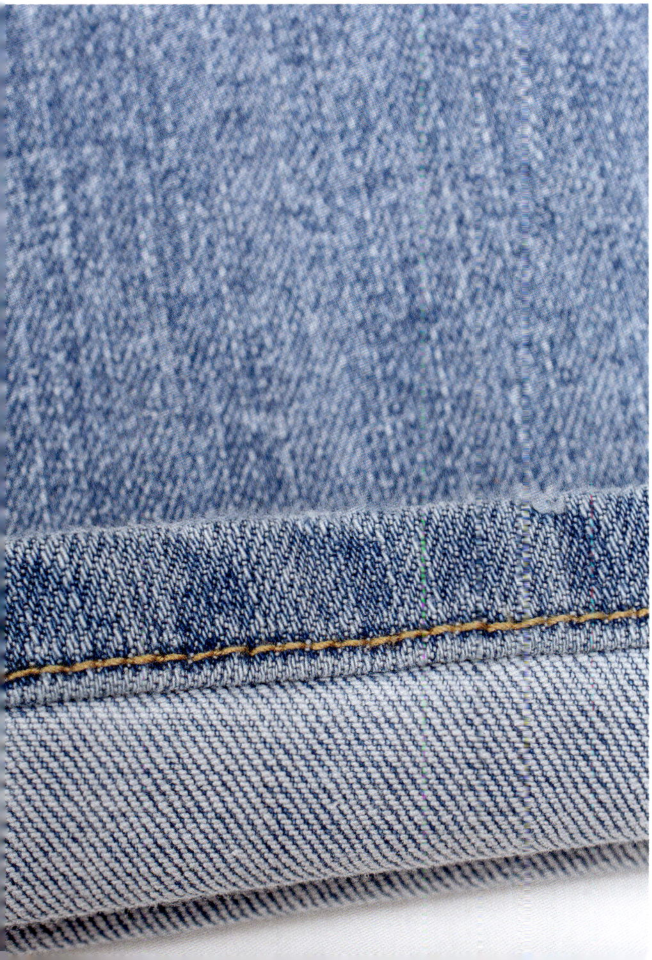
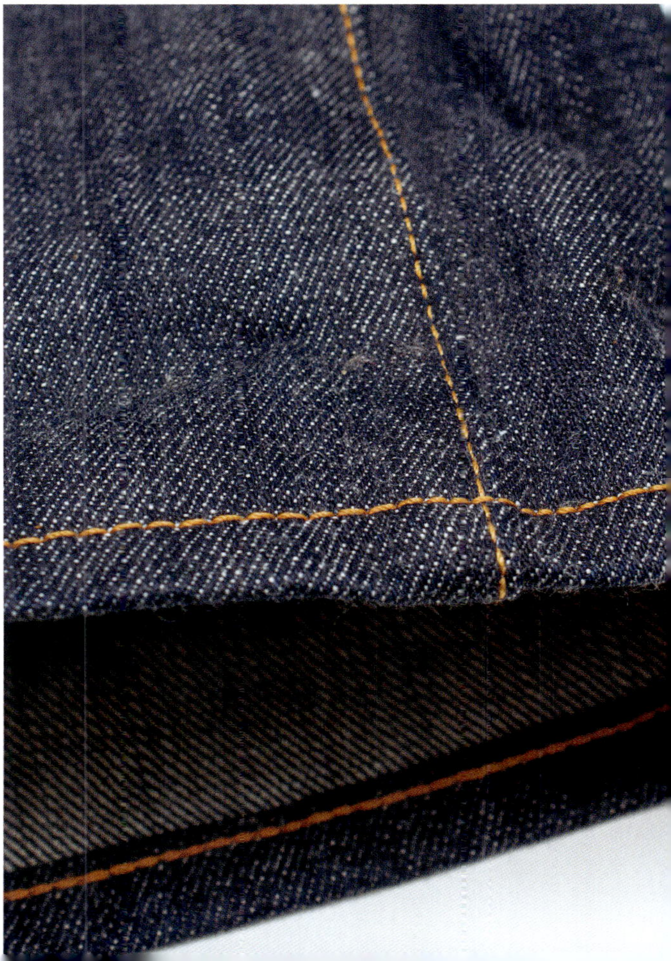

CHAPTER 6
DISTRESSING

THREADED HOLES

In this popular distressing technique, the holes are held together with white weft thread. Commonly used on knees and thighs but can be applied to any part of the jeans, including the pocket and hem area.

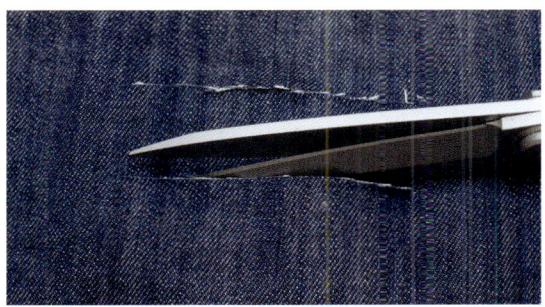

1 **Slash the distressed area.** Cut two parallel slashes through the fabric using a pair of scissors. Make the cuts as long as you want the distressed area to be.

2 **Remove the warp thread.** Using a pair of tweezers, remove the blue vertical warp threads that run between the slashed area. Start in one corner and pluck. The first few threads can be a bit hard to pull, but after that, they will loosen easily, as long as you pull the threads in order.

3 **Fray the edges.** Remove the white weft thread by inserting a needle and pulling the threads loose. You can either let the white threads hang or trim them down for a more even-looking edge.

4 **Soften the edges with a grater.** Another option is to rub the edges of the fabric against a grater using the raspy side. This will create a soft, naturally worn look.

OPEN HOLES

If you want ripped jeans with large holes, use this cut and fray method. Either leave the holes open or insert contrasting fabric underneath for a patched look.

1 Cut an opening. You can either do this straight or do more uneven cuts, depending on the look you want to have for the hole.

2 Distress the edges. Remove the warp thread on the vertical edges and the weft thread on the horizontal sides using a needle. It's common to let some of the white weft threads hang, whereas the blue warp threads are often removed.

3 Use a grater (optional). To soften the edges even more, rub them against the grater.

4 The finished hole. To get a really distressed look, remove several rows of thread. Another option is to slash the fabric unevenly.

FRAYED HEM

If you don't hem your jeans, the hem will start to fray eventually. But sometimes you might want to speed up the process or have already hemmed and want to give the jeans a more distressed look. By following this method you'll achieve fashionable frayed jeans in just a few minutes.

1 **Cut the leg.** Remember that, with fraying, the length of jeans will become even shorter.

2 **Remove the white weft thread.** Insert the needle and pull the threads loose. Keep pulling the weft threads until you are happy with the fraying.

3 **The finished hem.** You can either let the white threads hang or trim them down for a more even-looking edge.
TIP: Stitch a narrow straight stitch close to edge to prevent more fraying.

CHAPTER 7
TOOL KIT

DOWNLOAD THE JEANS PATTERN TOOL KIT

As a *Sewing Jeans* book bonus, you can download a free pattern tool kit to get access to pattern pieces and templates that will help you making even better jeans!

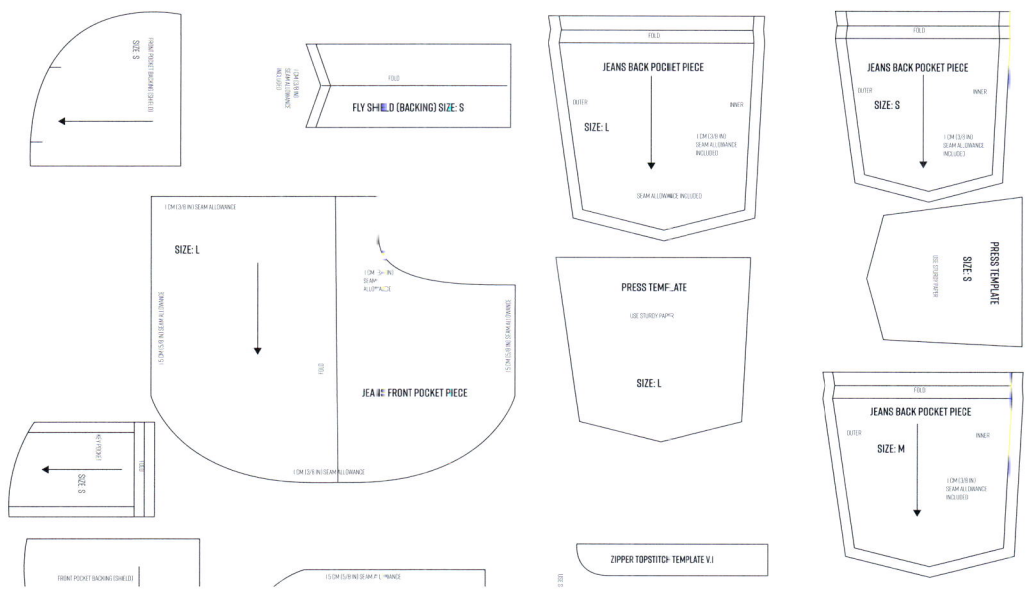

thelaststitch.com/jeansbookdownload

INCLUDED IN THE TOOL KIT

- Front pocket pattern pieces
- Back pocket pattern pieces
- Press and topstitching templates
- Zipper fly pattern pieces
- Button fly pattern pieces
- Back pocket topstitching templates

DOWNLOAD THE KIT

thelaststitch.com/jeansbookdownload

BACK POCKETS

The PDF Jeans Pattern Tool kit includes five different back pocket styles.

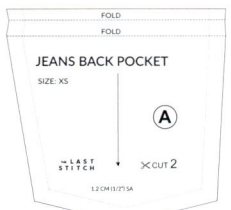
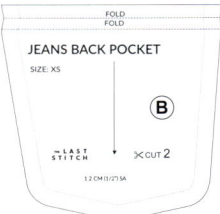
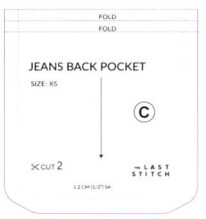
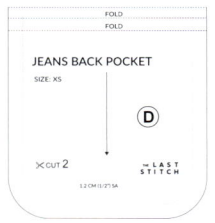
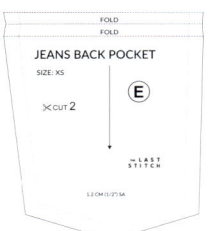

PLACEMENT OF ASYMMETRICAL POCKETS

Pocket styles A, B and E have asymmetrical slanted sides, meaning that the pockets are slanted slightly more on one side compared to the other. That is very common in the garment industry and is a way to create a distinct visual shaping to the area.

Usually, the most slanted side is placed towards the crotch seam, but play around with the placement and see what works for you.

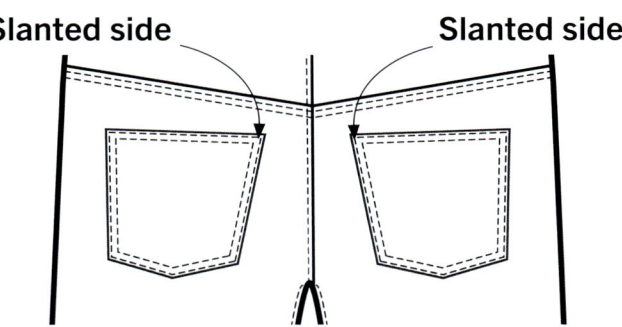

USING THE PRESS TEMPLATE

All sizes and versions of the back pocket patterns come with a corresponding press template (see page 111 for a demonstration). Retrace the press template on heavier card stock and press in the seam allowances around it.

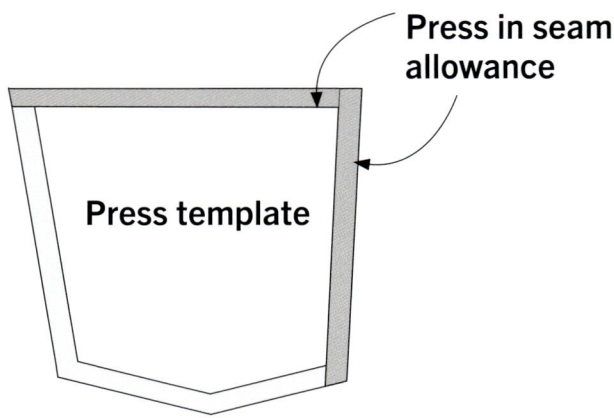

FLY PIECES

The button and zipper fly pattern pieces in the tool kit makes it easy to sew a professional button fly if your jeans pattern lacks this option.

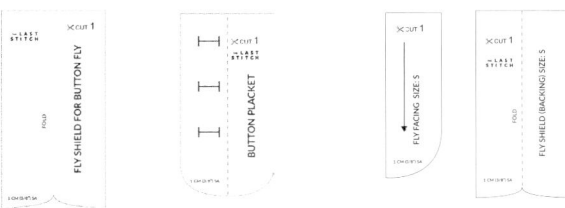

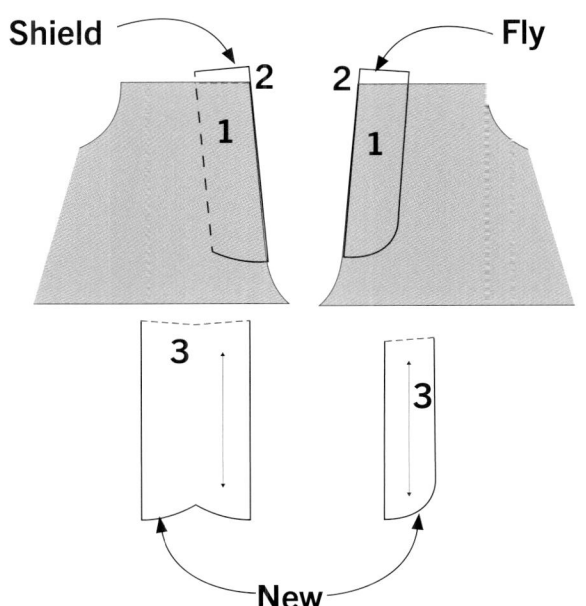

ADJUSTING THE FLY PIECES

The fly pieces are made extra long for easy trimming. Either trim them after sewing the fly together or adjust the pattern before sewing:

1. Place the extension facing and shield on the front jeans pattern piece and adjust the length so that it matches the zipper length or button fly that you plan to use.

2. If the front crotch is slanted, retrace the top of the shield and facing so that the pattern follows the shape of the crotch seam. Tip: Fold the shield before you retrace to make both layers even.

3. You can still cut the fly pattern pieces vertically with a grainline, even if the crotch is slanted.

MORE INSTRUCTIONS IN THE TOOL KIT

thelaststitch.com/jeansbookdownload

INDEX

A
Alterations
 bootcut jeans 29
 calves, tightness 36
 crotch folds 35
 crotch issues 32–35
 flared jeans 28
 flat bum 33
 full bum 32, 33
 gaping back 36
 guide to 37
 lengthen 35
 round tummy 34
 selvedge cut jeans 26
 shorten 35
 skinny jeans 27
 smiles 32
 sway back 34
 thin thighs 35
Assembly, order of 68

B
Back pockets 37
 decorative stitching 116–119
 pattern pieces 110, 185
 placements 114–115
 sewing 110–113
Bar tacks
 fly 99
 settings 64
 sewing 64–65
 thread 65
 tool 65
Belt loops
 attaching 154–158
 coverstitch, with attachment 148–149
 coverstitch, without attachment 146–147
 placement 154
 single stitch 150–152
 triple-layer, serged 142–143
 twin-needle 144–145

Bootcut jeans
 fabric for 15
 patterns for 29
Broken twill 11
Bull denim 14
Buttonholes
 marking and measuring 164
 needles 163
 sewing 163–165
 thread for 163
Buttons
 attaching 166–169
 donut 168–169
 flat top 166–167
 types 47

C
Chainstitch 173
Chambray 14
Coverstitch
 belt loops 146–147, 146–149
 hemming 173–176
 stitches for jeans 50
Cutting denim 20–21

D
Denim
 choosing fabric 15
 cutting 20–21
 definition 11
 denim, types of 11–14
 stretch 12
 sustainability 18–19
 washing and drying 16–17
 weave types 10–11
Distressing
 frayed hem 183
 open holes 182
 threaded holes 181

F
Fabric. *See* Denim
Fit. *See* Alterations

Flared jeans
 fabric for 15
 pattern for 28
Flat-felling
 flat-felling presser foot 42, 61–63
 guide to 56–57
 professional method 58–60
 seam allowances 57
 yoke and crotch seams 126–128
Fly
 button fly 100–107
 patterns for 84, 93, 100, 185
 professional zipper fly 84–92
 zipper fly with extension 93–99
Front pockets
 coin pocket, with 76–81
 pattern pieces 72, 76, 185
 regular 72–75

H
Hemming
 chainstitched 173–176
 frayed, distressing technique 183
 straight stitch 170–172
 triple straight stitch 177–178
Hemp denim 14
Hump-jumper 42, 54, 65, 127–128

I
Indigo 10
Interfacing
 fly, for 85, 96, 101
 types 47
 waistband, for 131, 136

L
Left-hand Twill 11

M
Marking
  awl 43
  chalk 97
  notches 21
  tracing paper 117

N
Needles
  denim 40
  topstitch 40
  twin-needle 40
Notions 46–47

O
Overcasting
  guide to 122
  stitches 50

P
Pattern tool kit 185
Pockets
  back pockets 110–119
  coin pocket 76–78
  front pockets 72–81
  lining 71, 72, 76
Presser feet
  buttonhole foot 41
  edge stitch foot 41
  flat-felling foot 42
  jeans foot 41
  standard foot 40
  topstitching, for 53
  zipper foot 41

R
Raw denim 12
Right-hand twill 11
Rivets
  attaching 160–162
  types 47

S
Seam allowances 25
Seams
  bar tacks 64–65
  coverstitch 50–51, 146–147, 148–149, 173–176
  flat-felled 58–63, 126–128
  French 80
  overcasting 122
  pressing 69
  serged 50
  sewing machine 50–51
  stitches, for jeans 50–51
  topstitching 52–55, 116–119
Selvedge denim
  cutting layout 20–21
  definition 12
  pattern adjustments 26
Serger
  seam finishes 50–51, 122, 142
Skinny jeans
  fabric for 15, 27
Stitches
  2-needle coverstitch 50
  3-thread overlock 50
  4-thread overlock 50
  5-thread safety stitch 51
  chainstitch 50
  straight stitch 50
  triple straight stitch 51
  twin-needle 51
  zigzag stitch 50
Stonewashed denim 13
Stretch denim 12
Sustainability
  eco-friendlier options 12–14, 19
  environmental impact 18–19

T
Tencel denim 12
Thread
  bar tacks, for 65
  heavy thread 46, 52
  overlock 46
  sewing machine thread 46, 53
  topstitching, for 52–53
  woolly nylon 46
Tools 43–44
Topstitching
  needles, for 54
  stitch settings 54–55
  techniques 52–55
  thread, for 52–53
  tools, for 53–54
Twin-needle 40, 51, 144–145

W
Waistband
  curved, pattern for 30–31
  curved, sewing 136–140
  cutting 130
  interfacing 131, 136
  rectangular, sewing 130–135
Warp 10
Washing
  drying 17
  how to 17
  pre-wash 16–17, 20
Weft 10

Y
Yoke
  alterations 36
  flat-felled 57, 126–128
  seam allowances 126
  seam allowances, for 25, 57
  sewing 123, 126–127

Z
Zippers
  jeans, for 47
  professional zipper, sewing 84–92
  zipper with fly extension, sewing 93–99

RESOURCES

> **SEWING JEANS RESOURCE COLLECTION**
>
> thelaststitch.com/sewingjeans
>
> The go-to place for all things sewing jeans and the companion resource for this book. List of jeans sewing patterns, denim and notion vendors, videos, jeans sewing tutorials and lots more.

BOOKS

Pattern fitting

Pants for Real People (Pati Palmer, Marta Alto)

The Complete Photo Guide to Perfect Fitting (Sarah Veblen)

Pattern making

Practical Guide to Patternmaking for Fashion Designers: Juniors, Misses and Women (Lori A. Knowles)

The Practical Guide to Patternmaking for Fashion Designers: Menswear (Lori A. Knowles)

Metric Pattern Cutting for Women's Wear (Winifred Aldrich)

Metric Pattern Cutting for Menswear (Winifred Aldrich)

Mending

Mending Matters: Stitch, Patch, and Repair Your Favorite Denim (Katrina Rodabaugh)

Jeans history and design

Denim Branded: Jeanswear's Evolving Design Details (Nick Williams)

True Fit: A Collected History of Denim (Viktor Fredback)

SEWING JEANS VIDEO COURSE

Denim Mastery: The Complete Video Guide To Sewing Your Own Jeans

Ready to level up your jeans-making skills? With the video sewing course Denim Mastery you learn how to sew jeans like a professional using your home sewing equipment.

The course guides you through the whole process of making jeans. The lessons are hands-on and visual, with lots of practical tips to help you follow along easily, no matter your skill level.

courses.thelaststitch.com

OTHER BOOKS BY JOHANNA LUNDSTRÖM

IMAGE ATTRIBUTIONS

All photos taken by Johanna Lundström and Anja Cederbom with the following exceptions:

Racool Studio / Freepik, 8, 17, 180: Freepik, 82–83, 108–109, 120: 123RF.com, 82–83, 108–109, 120, 153: Pixabay, 15, 16, 18